Grace under Pressure

Grace under Pressure

Negotiating the Heart of the Methodist Traditions

Joerg Rieger

General Board of Higher Education and Ministry
The United Methodist Church
Nashville, Tennessee

Contents

Acknowledgments

Some parts of this book have been published elsewhere as essays, but everything has been substantially reworked and updated for this book.

An earlier version of chapter 1 was published as "What Do Margins and Center Have to Do with Each Other? The Future of Methodist Traditions and Theology," in Joerg Rieger and John Vincent, eds., *Methodist and Radical: Rejuvenating a Tradition* (Nashville: Kingswood Books, 2003). The basic ideas of chapter 2 began as an essay titled "Between God and the Poor: Rethinking the Means of Grace in the Wesleyan Tradition," in Richard P. Heitzenrater, ed., *The Poor and the People Called Methodists* (Nashville: Kingswood Books, 2002), 83–99. Written permission to reproduce these two essays here is gratefully acknowledged.

An earlier version of chapter 3 was published as "Beyond Burnout: New Creation and the Economics of Grace in Global Capitalism," *Quarterly Review* 24, no. 1 (Spring 2004): 67–79. (*Quarterly Review* is a publication of the General Board of Higher Education and Ministry, The United Methodist Church.)

Earlier versions of chapter 4 were published as "Methodism and Empire: The Beginnings," *Revista Caminhando* 13, no. 2 (July–December 2008): 124–30; and "Methodism and Empire: The Nineteenth and Twentieth Centuries," *Revista Caminhando* 14 no. 1 (January–June 2009): 93–104 (online at www.metodista.br/revistas/revistas-metodista/index.php/CA). *Revista Caminhando* is a scientific journal and is an open-access publication of the Faculty of Theology of the United Methodist Church, located at the Methodist University of São Paolo, Brazil. Permission to use these articles is greatly appreciated.

Parts of the conclusion were published as "Globalization, Empire, and Beyond: The Pitfalls and Promises of a Global Church," *Occasional Paper,* #101 (Nashville: General Board of Higher Education and Ministry, The United Methodist Church, December 2008); other parts were initially published in "The Word of God and the People of God: Revitalizing Theological Discourse from the Bottom Up," *Quarterly Review* 21, no. 2 (Spring 2001): 33–44.

| Introduction |

Missing the Reality of Grace in the Church

CHRISTIANITY IS NOT PRIMARILY ABOUT RELIGION OR MORALITY. It is about what I am calling here "grace under pressure." Within Christianity, the Methodist traditions have embodied this insight in powerful ways, although it has often been neglected or gone unrecognized. At the heart of these traditions lies the insight that the divine is more authentically experienced in the midst of the pressures of life than on the mountaintops. Today this insight is shared by many people around the globe, especially those who struggle for liberation and for survival. Without this insight, Christianity is prone to miss the reality of grace and the ability to see the real difference that God makes in the world. This is not just a problem for Methodism; it is one of the core problems of mainline Christianity today.

When mainline Christians consider the pressures of life, they often see these as individual and isolated incidences that are of no consequence in the long run. They don't recognize how these pressures contribute to the bigger picture. Yet many of the pressures of our time are so stark that they have become matters of life and death. More and more lives are ruined and lost, for instance, in the midst of economic struggles that are not only reflected in the growing gap between the richest and the poorest, but also increasingly extend to those who consider themselves to be middle class.[1] Lives are destroyed, too, in the midst of asymmetries of power in both personal and global relationships. Domestic abuse at home, abuses of power in the workplace and in international relations—all have taken on epidemic pro-portions. Tensions along the lines of class, gender, and sexuality, as well as tensions along the lines of race and ethnicity, also have taken on a life-and-death urgency. These matters ultimately affect us all, whoever and wherever we are. Furthermore, they are genuine matters of faith. Dealing with them is the challenge at the very heart of Christianity. It is what makes the church the church. The United Methodist *Book of Discipline* puts the challenge in these words: "Realities of intense human suffering, threats to the survival of life, and challenges to human dignity confront us afresh with fundamental theological issues."[2]

God's grace comes alive in powerful ways in the midst of those pressures. In fact, it is most active under pressure. That is perhaps one of Christianity's most powerful insights. It has taken on shape at various points throughout Christian history; yet it seems that the Methodist movements have experienced this ir-repressible grace in especially powerful ways. As a result, the Methodist traditions can provide deeper insights into how grace works under pressure, not just for their own benefit but also for the benefit of Christianity and of the world as a whole.

These insights need to be tested and applied in the context of the following question: how does grace under pressure challenge and transform the pressures of our times, lead us beyond the self-centeredness of much church life, and produce new hope for both church and world? Or, in simpler terms: what difference, if any, does Christianity make in the midst of the real pressures of life? This question haunts more and more of us every day.

The concerns of this book, therefore, are practical, concluding with some reflections on new models of leadership that challenge most of what is presented as the logic of leadership today. In this sense, this book can be read as an outline of the relevance of the Methodist traditions for the challenges of both church and world today, and the difference they might make. At the same time, the book can also be read as a theology of grace, and an effort to rethink the core of the Methodist heritage in light of its contributions for Christianity as a whole.

Religious Self-Centeredness

For the most part, religion appears to be going strong in the United States. Nevertheless, a crisis looming on the horizon has to do with a pervasive self-centeredness that, while occasionally interrupted by churches' efforts at what is called outreach, tends to focus most of our time and attention on internal matters. One harmful result is a gradual loss of faith, as faith shrivels when it becomes self-centered and self-referential. Another result is the loss of some of the most faithful church members. Many are beginning to sense that the church is playing what amounts to pious sandbox games. And even when religion engages the public sphere, self-centeredness often remains an issue; the so-called gospel of prosperity promises individual success in life to the pious rather than hope for the masses. The phrase *God bless America*, which keeps resurfacing especially in times of pressure, also promotes self-centeredness; it tends to tie God to our own concerns and to the concerns of people like us. Members of mainline churches may consider these two examples extreme, and self-centeredness might not be promoted quite so blatantly in those churches as elsewhere, but these churches are not exempt from self-centeredness. Therefore, rethinking the Methodist traditions may bring relief not only to Methodism but also to mainline Christianity as a whole. What is perhaps most impressive about the early Methodist traditions is that, back then, religion occasionally managed to break out of the self-centeredness of its own time. The hope is that this might teach us some valuable lessons for how we can break out of the self-centeredness of our times.

Then and now, breaking out of religious self-centeredness is based on a two-fold challenge: how do we deal with our neighbors, and how do we deal with God? Self-centered religion fails on each of these counts, and John Wesley kept wrestling with both issues throughout his life. For the sake of providing a clear contrast, compare the common take on poverty, then and now, with Wesley's view on poverty. Based on the "American Dream," according to which anyone can climb the ladder of success, many Christians in the United States today assume that poverty has to do with the personal failure of people who are poor. Blaming the poor has become the default mode even in the churches. This attitude has become so pervasive that it even shapes the self-perception of many poor people.

Wesley encountered similar attitudes in his own time, but he proposed a different perspective and a new relation to the poor. He pointed out that poverty was closely related to the behavior of the rich and to structural economic matters that favored the wealthy (see chapter 1). At first sight, this matter might appear to be a minor issue for Christianity. Yet, as will become increasingly clearer throughout the book, the heart of the Christian faith is negotiated to a large degree by how we relate to our neighbors, and these relations become most visible when we look at how we relate to those of our neighbors who have been pushed to the margins. Religious narcissism can be challenged only when we begin to relate to others in new ways and begin to see the world from their perspective, rather than from our own.

The second question has to do with how we approach God. The way we relate to other people mirrors the way we relate to God. Self-centered religion that views other people in its terms is likely to view the divine in its terms as well. As a result, both others and the divine Other are shaped in the dominant image. This problem is quite widespread: God is commonly defined in terms of those whom we consider to be powerful and successful. And even those who would assert "God is everywhere" need to ask themselves: where do you look for God in times of great pressure and need? The default position, it seems, is to look for God at the top. This is a constant temptation, and it appears to have been a problem in the Methodist movements as well. When Wesley complained, for instance, that people who improved their social standing with the help of Methodism never stopped to look back, one wonders whether this problem might not ultimately point to a theological deficit. If God is not found at the bottom of society, what motivation would Methodists and other Christians have to take seriously life at the bottom of society after they have climbed the ladder of success?

What went wrong at times in the Methodist movement itself, it might be argued, is that self-centeredness reemerged due to a failure to clarify the character of God. Most of the chapters that follow quote Wesley's surprising claim that "religion must not go from the greatest to the least, or the power would appear to be of men." Our task is to combine Wesley's claim about religion with a fresh understanding of the character of God, as top-down religion goes hand in glove with top-down images of God. The alternative—religion that moves from the bottom up—requires bottom-up images of God. The good news is that we do not have to start from scratch in arguing our case: the Christian traditions, as will become clear in the pages to come, are full of divine images that move from the bottom up.

The core problem is, therefore, not first of all what has often been called practical atheism: faith that does not lead to a change in a person's life and to a personal connection with God. Wesley himself noted that this faith was misguided.[3] However, the bigger problem, then and now, seems to be what might be called a misguided theism, a self-centered understanding of God that is tied up with a self-centered way of life. What if self-centered Christianity was indeed acting on its beliefs? Much more than Wesley was able to see in his day, we need to rethink our images of God along with rethinking our images of our neighbors. This is especially important in a context of top-down power, where everyone assumes by default that this is how God works as well: from the top down.

Taking a cue from Wesley, we are thus pushing beyond some of his fundamental insights. Yet the goal remains the same: how can we make sure that Christianity is renewed in such a way that it reflects the all-transforming power of God, rather than the powers that be? What is at stake here, to be sure, is not a minor improvement of Christianity. What is at stake is nothing less than the future of the church itself.

A Road Map of the Project

Ernest Hemingway is credited with the notion of "grace under pressure,"[4] yet some of the Methodist traditions embody this dynamic. In chapter 1 we will see that Methodism, since the days of John Wesley, has been most alive, creative, and productive when it has dealt with situations of pressure. Wesley's insight that "religion must not go from the greatest to the least" places Christianity squarely in the midst of the pressures of everyday life. The primary focus of this move is not on social action, as is commonly assumed, but on new experiences of grace under pressure. In the process, new energy emerges, new encounters with God happen, and both church and world are transformed.

Chapter 2 provides the theological core of the book. It investigates the wide-ranging implications of the fact that John Wesley included what he called "works of mercy" into the classical means-of-grace tradition. This move changes both the means-of-grace tradition and the nature of works of mercy and social action: no longer primarily projects of "outreach," they become places of God's "inreach." Thus they reflect God's transformation of Christianity and the world in solidarity with people at the margins and under pressure. Wesley was concerned that many Methodists had fallen from grace because they neglected works of mercy as means of grace. If he was right about this, paying attention to this concern is decisive for the future of the church. When we introduce works of mercy into the means-of-grace tradition, a new dynamic develops that affects the other means of grace as well: we read the Bible with new eyes; prayer is no longer a self-centered enterprise; Holy Communion opens up to include the "least of these." This may well be the most distinct and constructive contribution of Methodism to the future of theology and the church, with tremendous implications for the world.

Chapters 3 and 4 work through the theological theme of grace in terms of two of the most pressing issues of our time that have become matters of life and death. Chapter 3 develops the implications of the Methodist traditions for economic issues, which deeply concerned Wesley. Based on what I call Wesley's "alternative economics of grace," the Methodist traditions not only contain some challenges for the status quo of the free-market economy; these traditions also hold out hope for alternative economic relations and help to develop alternative models that radically transform how we relate to one another, both in the church and in the world. A radically new relation to God, that pushes beyond what is imagined possible in mainline Christianity, is at the heart of it all.

The question of the relation of church and theology to empire and colonialism is relatively new, although Christianity has been shaped by empires from its very beginnings. In chapter 4, I explore how Methodism has developed in the context of empire, yet keeps pointing beyond empire. Although early Methodism cannot be seen in isolation from the benefits of the British Empire and the expanding United States, Methodism also provided alternatives that made a difference. One of the most important questions for Christianity today is rooted in this heritage: is God bigger than contemporary efforts at building empires? Unless this is clear, those who recognize Christianity's incompatibility with empire will continue to leave the church in disappointment, while those who support empire remain stuck in the common confusion of God and the powers that be. The good news is that even in this situation "grace under pressure" points us to alternatives that can create real hope today.

When I tell my students "theology is a matter of life and death," I am not talking about the importance of my field in the academy. History teaches us that theology has functioned in both ways, as life affirming and as death dealing. In this book, I examine how a theology of grace can be life affirming even in the midst of great pressures that seem insurmountable. Key to this renewed vision of grace is God's own work in both church and world, preceding and empowering fresh ways of human action, human hope, and human belief: this action makes a difference where we least expect it—continuously moving not from the greatest to the least but the other way around. Nothing less than the future of the church—and the world—depends on this.

| Chapter 1 |

Methodism Thriving under Pressure

AS STATED EARLIER, WHILE ERNEST HEMINGWAY RECEIVES THE credit for coming up with the phrase "grace under pressure," Methodism can be seen as an embodiment of this dynamic. Methodism, since the days of John Wesley, has been most alive, creative, and productive when it dealt with situations of pressure. When Methodism placed itself squarely in the midst of the pressures of everyday life, new experiences of grace under pressure materialized, new encounters with God took place, and both church and world were transformed.

Methodism in the twenty-first century has become mainline in most places around the globe and, as an unfortunate consequence, has withdrawn from its engagement with situations of pressure. This is not to say that the mainline would not also experience situations of pressure; but the mainline has developed strategies for avoiding these pressures as much as possible, or at least for avoiding encounters with their deeper roots.

In the United States, United Methodism is representative of mainline Protestantism, as it constitutes the nation's second-largest Protestant denomination. But even in places where Methodism holds the status of a minute minority, such as in Europe, it has often become respectable and moved in sync with the mainline denominations. Even Methodism that is more dynamic, emerging in many places in Asia and Africa, often tends to understand itself as part of the more established Protestant denominations. The history of Methodism is often told in similar terms. This is how it goes: those blue-collar workers of early European industrialization who made up the early Methodist communities in Britain, together with the poor and other marginalized groups, became upwardly mobile and in this way embodied the positive influence and success of Methodism. Moreover, Methodism prevented revolutionary bloodshed in England, some claim, because it helped to lift many members of the lower classes out of their misery.[1] Situations of pressure, this scenario implies, were exchanged for the relative bliss of a mainline middle-class existence and an increasing concern with the finer things of life. That John Wesley was quite wary of such forms of success is another story that, if remembered at all, is often told in a moralizing tone that has little to do with deeper structural or theological issues.

Becoming part of the mainline, the Methodist churches' concern for situations of pressure as they are experienced especially at the margins of society has declined. Yet part of the power of the early Methodist movement lay precisely in the fact that it was not a movement of the mainline and that it mustered the courage to deal with the pressures experienced at the margins.[2] What little remains of our concern for the margins in Methodism now usually follows this narrative: we Methodists have made it, and we want others to make it, too. In this context, our concern for the margins is reduced to a matter of service to the disadvantaged, as the sense for the most acute pressures of life and their causes has been lost. All that remains to be done, the mainline assumes, is to provide a chance for others to become more like us.

It is not surprising that Methodism has its own variation of the "from rags to riches" story. We live, after all, in a globalizing economy that measures success in terms of numbers, services performed, monetary value, and professional accomplishment. The question to be addressed in the chapters of this book, however, is: what would it mean, *precisely in this context,* to recover a connection to the real pressures of life and to the particular forms of grace experienced in these pressures?

Beyond the Middle Road

Usually the mainline derives its authority either directly through majority vote or through the invention of a theological and political "middle road," which operates on the basis of a lowest common denominator. Whatever does not fit these categories is quickly classified as "extremist." Of interest is only what can somehow be integrated into the lowest common denominator. As a result, the mainline considers the concerns of the margins and the pressures experienced in this context only as long as they fit the middle road of the lowest common denominator. In the racial confrontation between black and white in the United States, for instance, the "centrist" middle road appears to lie somewhere between whites who are explicitly racist and blacks who argue for separation and autonomy. The tensions between rich and poor provide a similar example: the mainline invents itself somewhere in the vast space between the very rich and the very poor, commonly dubbed the "middle" class. In the United States, most people are led to believe that they belong somewhere in the middle, and that they thus reside at a safe distance from the most extreme pressures of life. What brings people together in this middle realm and what creates cohesion is the resistance to the extremes. In this situation, the pressures experienced by the middle are covered up and repressed, and the deeper pressures of life—endured especially by those who reside at the margins in terms of race and class (to stay within our example)—never even show up.

No wonder that the mainline never harbors the slightest doubt that its own discourse defines what is of common interest. From this perspective, voices from the margins—if they are recognized at all—appear to represent mainly special interests. The only place where the mainline really needs to pay attention is where there may be overlaps. Where people on the margins want what everybody else wants, the mainline picks up steam and thus may grant some justification to their concerns. But what if things were precisely the other way around? What if not the mainline but the margins were able to grasp what really matters, due to the fact that the margins are more immediately in touch with the deeper pressures of life? This question has implications far beyond the Methodist movements.

The trouble with locating common interest with the majority is that what is considered to be the majority will predetermine the outcome; the deeper pressures of life will likely be lost—and with it the opportunity to experience grace under pressure that concerns us here. The majority of theologians in the middle of the twentieth century, for instance, had little disagreement about what it meant to be human. But back then the international and ecumenical community of most theologians also happened to be made up primarily of middle-class white men who displayed little awareness of the great battles for life and survival of the time.[3] By the same token, the majority of delegates to the General Confer-ence of The United Methodist Church still do not represent the gender and racial identity of the membership of our churches and the related pressures, even though there is some improvement to report. But even if gender and racial bal-ance were achieved, the factor of class remains. When determining questions of majority, we need to remind ourselves that since the majority of the membership of The United Methodist Church in the United States is middle class, we do not represent the socioeconomic pressures experienced by the majority of Methodists around the world—or even the majority of Christians in the United States itself, let alone the majority of world Christianity.

When common interest is located with the lowest common denominator, things are watered down and a sense for the most acute pressures of life is lost. United Methodist theologian Albert Outler's often-repeated claim that Wesley promoted a "high-church evangelicalism," for instance, can easily be used to argue that one can (and perhaps even should) have it both ways—be both "high church" and evangelical—in terms of a lowest common denominator. As a result, every-thing stays the same; nothing is challenged or transformed, and everybody is kept happy, except of course those who refuse to "have it both ways" and are thus considered "extremists."[4] Worse yet, the lowest common denominator will be determined to a large degree by those whom we consider to be the major players. When the lowest common denominator is determined, for example, in the tension between mainline conservatives and their liberal counterparts, this tension is used to classify the concerns of everybody else—even though most people may not care much about it. This is indeed what has happened in the United States; we have not yet quite realized that the concerns of those who do not fit the dominant liberal–conservative paradigm, such as African Americans, Hispanics, Asians, lower-class people, and people in other parts of the world, cannot really be understood in terms of the dominant paradigm.[5] There is indeed little common interest here.

John Wesley himself seems to have had some sense of the dangers of this "mainlining" or "mainstreaming" of Christianity. In a sermon about the image of the broad and the narrow way in the Gospel of Matthew, he put it like this: "Are there many wise, many rich, many mighty or noble, travelling with you in the same way? By this token, without going any farther, you know it does not lead to life."[6] The problem with the mainline—with the multitudes who walk in the broad way—is not that they lack perfection or display some moral shortcomings;

this is true of all human beings. There is a more fundamental problem: the logic of the mainline, of the powers that be, does not lead to life and is fundamentally flawed. In Wesley's unmistakable words: "If you are walking as the generality of men walk, you are walking to the bottomless pit."[7]

If the mainline is thus fundamentally flawed, what happens if we take a look at the margins? Here a curious reversal takes place between common interest and special interests. Contrary to the logic of the mainline, the pressures experienced in full force by people on the margins are not matters of special interest. In the words of the apostle Paul, "If one member suffers, all suffer together with it" (1 Cor. 12:26). Moreover, Paul—not unlike Wesley—seems to have understood that those members who consider themselves superior due to their position of privilege are the real promoters of special interests. In Paul's words: "The eye cannot say to the hand, 'I have no need of you,' nor again the head to the feet, 'I have no need of you.' On the contrary, the members of the body that seem to be weaker are indispensable" (1 Cor. 12:21–22). But does this also mean that we can actually learn something from the pressures experienced at the margins?[8] And what would that be?

Unlike the concerns of the mainline and of privilege, the pressures experienced by people marginalized because of issues such as race, gender, sexuality, or class include awareness of the extremes and therefore of the deeper pressures of life that ultimately affect us all. For example, the pressures experienced by marginalized women include men as those who marginalize. The pressures experienced by marginalized African Americans include European Americans as those who benefit from this marginalization, whether they intend to or not. The pressures experienced by marginalized people living in poverty include a sense that the rich, or even the middle class, are not off the hook. The dominant groups, on the other hand, usually are less aware of these relationships and thus they often neglect the deeper pressures of life; at times these relationships and pressures are covered up altogether. The myth of individualism, for instance, at the heart of our contemporary belief systems, even in the church, suggests that those who are on top have pulled themselves up by their own bootstraps, and that they have earned their escape from the worst pressures of life. This myth serves as a cover-up for the reality that the identity of those on top is produced in relation to others and oftentimes on the backs of others—in situations of extreme pressure from which one side benefits and the other does not.

Wesley took a first step beyond his own position of privilege when, in visiting the sick and the poor, he began to understand, for example, that poverty is usually not the fault of the poor[9]—a common assumption then and now. In the process, he realized that becoming aware of the pressures the poor have to endure can teach us something about privilege and the powers that be.[10] With this seemingly small step, he opened the way for a whole new set of questions, for a broader horizon, and for an exploration of new forms of consciousness in touch with the margins and the deeper pressures of life. A genuine experience of grace under pressure was the result as the Methodist movement took off. Could something akin to a new awakening be the result of our taking similarly small steps in our own context that push beyond our own position of privilege and put us in touch with the deeper pressures of our time?

"Religion Must Not Go from the Greatest to the Least"

In a May 21, 1764, journal entry, Wesley stated, "Religion must not go from the greatest to the least, or the power would appear to be of men."[11] Almost two decades later, in 1783, Wesley expressed this insight the other way around: "'They shall all know me,' saith the Lord, not from the greatest to the least (this is that wisdom of the world which is foolishness with God) but 'from the least to the greatest,' that the praise may not be of men, but of God."[12] These insights point us to new encounters with grace under pressure.

Of course, in mainline Methodism we have not given much thought to which way "religion goes." But a closer look reveals that our normal approach runs counter to Wesley's intuition. Our efforts to proclaim the good news in word and deed tend to move indeed "from the greatest to the least," from those who are better endowed with power and money to those who have less. Yet in following this approach we have missed out on vital encounters with grace under pressure.

For instance, what has been called "urban ministry" often takes the shape of suburban churches and urban strategists reclaiming the cities through so-called outreach ministries, which include after-school programs, building projects, and food pantries. Through these activities we somehow feel that we are now bringing God back to the cities, as if God also left when the Methodist churches joined the white flight from the cities since the 1960s. But what if God did not leave the city when the churches left? If God is still at work at the margins and in the midst of the deeper pressures of life, religion no longer has to go from the greatest to the least, and a new thing may happen.

As some Perkins School of Theology faculty and students learned when we began building relationships with people in West Dallas—a part of town severely marginalized along the lines of race and class—meeting God in West Dallas can change your life. Little did we know back then that this was only the beginning; these incidents led to experiences of God in the midst of a globalizing economy and the pressures of what we would later call "empire." During the past decade, we have continued to engage in issues of labor and religion, particularly through the activities of North Texas Jobs with Justice.[13]

The now-abandoned United Methodist Bishops' Initiative on Children and Poverty faced a similar challenge.[14] Despite the bishops' clear conclusion that we do not need first of all more programs and emphases, and that what is at stake is "nothing less than the reshaping of The United Methodist Church in response to the God who is among 'the least of these,'" most churches and annual conferences continue to move from the greatest to the least.[15] When confronted with the pressures experienced by children in poverty, the reaction was almost always the same: how can we help them? This shows once more our tacit assumption-turned-common-sense that the normal flow of things is indeed from the greatest to the least—and from situations of lower to situations of higher pressure. Based on the logic of the mainline, even the now-common expression of "working with" rather than "working for" those in need will not necessarily reverse the movement from the top down and leaves those at the top unchallenged. At this point in time, mainline churches do not really have any alternative modes of dealing with the deeper pressures of life.

The two camps within the mainline—the liberal and the conservative—do not differ much when it comes to the pressures experienced by "the least of these." Liberals tend to favor social programs designed to take care of societal pressures that are so tremendous that they leave people stranded; conservatives tend to put more emphasis on personal responsibility and character formation. In both cases, the movement still is from the top down, seeking to "lift up" people on the margins. Both social programs and efforts at character formation are primarily designed to help those who have fallen through the cracks to find their way back into the system. Their goal is to relieve and mitigate pressure without investigating its deeper origins. This is true even for the somewhat more radical idea of "community organizing." In all those examples, success is defined by those who have made it up the social ladder and who can therefore afford to treat pressure in more casual ways. It is no wonder, therefore, that "the power would appear to be of men." The critics of this form of Christianity have had little difficulty in pointing out that, for the most part, God is no longer required here.[16] Religion fueled by those who are successful plays its own sort of role: in modern capitalist societies, those on the receiving end are led to believe that anybody can make it, with the result of playing down the pressures they experience on a daily basis. Those who give to people in need, on the other hand, are led to believe that they have earned every penny, while those who experience pressures have brought their misery on themselves. God is really not needed here, except to back up and justify the powers that be.

The bigger picture shows similar structures. Western Christianity has frequently moved right along with the successes and evolutions of that which has come to epitomize Western power: the economic system of free-market capitalism. From the conquest of the Americas with fire and sword in the search for gold to the colonialisms of the nineteenth century that secured raw materials and the production of simple goods for the center, Christianity has often spread parallel to the expansion of the economic and political powers that be. Now, in the era of global capitalism, Christianity has added a few more subtle moves through the use of new technologies such as the Internet, satellite, and other media, and so— still on the heels of the flow of money—religion continues to move from the greatest to the least. It is indeed not hard to notice whose power is at work here.

What happens, however, when religion moves the other way around? Mainline Christianity—and even its critics—has a hard time acknowledging that this can ever be the case.[17] What would the margins have to teach the mainline? The move from the bottom up opens the view for a whole new world that is full of miracles and surprises, where grace is experienced under pressure in new ways, and where the power no longer appears to "be of men." Mainline critics of religion will have a more difficult time explaining and dismissing these phenomena. Most of them are, of course, not likely to notice them anyway, together with mainline theologians and leaders of the church. But what if God is at work precisely where we least expect it—where the pressures of life are greatest? How could mainline theology and religion ever have seriously expected that

God would hook up with those in positions of acute pressure, like a small, insignificant tribe in the Middle East such as the people of Israel, the bands and classes of uneducated Methodists in industrializing Britain, or people today whose existence we hardly recognize because we have rendered them invisible even where they live right in our own midst?

Yet this new direction of Christianity can sometimes be glimpsed even within the mainline itself. For example, when North American church groups take mission trips to inner cities or to other places of pressure around the world, new encounters with God and other people sometimes occur, with the potential to help us break out of our religious narcissism. Unexpected and strange, these encounters cannot easily be done away with. A common reaction of the mainline is to ignore the challenge by playing down the pressures and celebrating what it knows: the success of its missionary heroes and its own generosity in helping others. This strategy still tends to be highly effective, and thus the challenges posed by these deeper pressures can usually be averted. But what remains is at least a barb in the hearts of those who have experienced God and other people in new ways. We ignore this at our own peril.

In this context, theology that begins to recognize these issues can make a tremendous difference by dealing with the deeper pressures of life, by paying the sort of attention that these pressures deserve, and by developing new tools to rethink the Christian tradition as a whole in this light. Here, theology in the Methodist tradition may find a new start in relation to what is already happening in some of our communities.[18]

Challenges to the Mainline

In the spring of 2001, the United Methodist bishops reaffirmed their earlier conclusion about children and poverty: "We are convinced that the reshaping of the church and the proclamation of the gospel cannot take place apart from a newly developed sense of community: that is, relationship of the church, including the bishops, with the economically impoverished and the most vulnerable of God's children. God has chosen the poor, the vulnerable, and the powerless as a means of grace and transformation."[19]

If we are serious about this move—which the bishops backed up earlier by a full-fledged theological argument that included references to Jesus' own way of relating to people on the margins and to the core of the Methodist tradition—can this amount to anything less than a reformation of the church? Unlike the Protestant Reformation of the sixteenth century, this reformation will not be accomplished by a few brilliant leaders. Rather, it needs to develop in community, from the bottom up and in touch with the real pressures of life. It will not be driven by ecclesial and religious professionals and their connections to the powers that be but will draw a new kind of energy that can grow only out of the experience of grace under pressure.

In this context the Wesleyan understanding of the means of grace, which will be discussed in more detail in the next chapter, provides a first step. Means of grace are channels through which we receive God's grace into our lives. One of Wesley's major achievements was that he expanded the traditional Anglican list of means of grace, which included prayer, Bible study, and Holy Communion, by adding what he called "works of mercy." This changes the conventional understanding of works of mercy. As channels of God's grace, works of mercy have an impact not only on those who receive them but also on those who do them. We must no longer talk about such works of mercy as charitable "outreach" activities, by which the "haves" touch the lives of the "have-nots." Works of mercy become tools of what for lack of a better word might be called "inreach"—tools for the reformation of the mainline church and, by extension, of the powers that be. This poses a radical challenge to the mainline that needs to be explored further.

What do we make of the fact that God reaches into our lives when we relate to people on the margins and under pressure? Even those of us who, not unlike Wesley, have developed relations with the margins in situations of great pressure still need to learn a few lessons. The biggest problem is the patronizing touch that has often accompanied works of mercy. God's grace is not to be found first of all in our status and prestige but under pressure—in the ways that we relate to others and others relate to us in situations of pressure. Moreover, works of mercy—such as praying, reading the Bible, or participating in Holy Communion—become channels for God to transform who we are. Those who read the Bible, for instance, know that it still has the potential to mess up the playgrounds of the theologians and the church at times.[20] Works of mercy, when seen as the points where God's grace reshapes our lives under pressure, have similar potential.

The Methodist tradition of the "open" Communion table provides another reference point for a renewed theology and church. Holy Communion is not the place where the pious few meet in a safe retreat from the pressures of the world. It is rather the place where people experience God's grace in the midst of situations of pressure, and where, in these situations, they seek to be forgiven and to live in peace with one another.[21] Wesley assumed that even people who were not yet Christians could benefit from participating in Holy Communion if they were in the process of responding to God's grace in their lives.[22] If God's grace is open to all and at work in situations of pressure where the mainline church (now and in Wesley's day) least expects it, then Holy Communion cannot be a closed event. Encountering God's presence at the Communion table is, therefore, closely tied to making peace with one another in situations of pressure—something that cannot happen without those people who are experiencing the pressures of what at times appears as a veritable warfare along the lines of race, class, and gender. What would happen if we truly opened our Communion tables in these ways? Would not making peace with those whom we keep at the margins and against whom we wage a different kind of war—often without even realizing it, since we may never meet them in person—lead to a major transformation of the church as a whole?

In all these examples a sense for the deeper pressures of life helps us gain a more profound understanding of who we are and of what we are up against in the twenty-first century. The main challenge for Methodism is not so much the inevitable process of institutionalization or the much-lamented lack of relevance. It is that, in our efforts to maintain stature, we are being sucked into the powers that be, which are now defined by the structures of global capitalism—an economic system that magnifies the pressures on larger and larger parts of the population and marginalizes them. Inequalities are becoming more severe. We even witness a new system of slavery that is more heinous than what Wesley could have imagined and more cruel than European and American slave trades ever were, since people have become more commodified than ever.[23] The gap between rich and poor continues to rise dramatically, globally as well as within the United States.[24] To maintain a mainline position in this situation usually means to find some middle ground—a position that, as I have argued above, is easily pulled in by the powers that be.

In this situation, a reformation "from below," in touch with the pressures of life, might have the potential of pushing beyond the mainline denominations and uniting large groups of Christians in new ways, where unity no longer runs counter to diversity. A broader horizon emerges at this point: the move to incorporate the deeper pressures of life does not narrow things down to the lowest common denominator but helps to broaden our view by recognizing what holds us together across the dividing lines of race, class, gender, denomination, and nationality, by reaching all the way down to the common roots of the pressures that we are experiencing around the globe. In view of these roots, new relations can be built that resist the logic of mainline Protestantism by valuing diversity and by requiring those who join in to understand who they are in relation to the pressures experienced by others—including the ones considered extreme.

The Theological Task

Methodists have long been proud of the fact that their faith and their theology are inextricably connected to the practical concerns of the Christian life. As we become more aware of the deeper pressures of life as a whole, our vision of the Christian life broadens as well. We can no longer merely zero in on some amorphous middle road and assume that this will provide the context of faith and theological reflection. While Methodist theology has traditionally sought to reflect on God in relation to humanity and the world, we now need to learn what it means to reflect on God in relation to a humanity and a world that are identified by acute pressures. Methodist theology needs to be done more self-consciously in the pressures that are located between God and the excluded,[25] and between what we have traditionally called "works of piety" and "works of mercy."

The traditional resources of Christian theology, including the Bible and the Christian traditions, need to be understood in relation to who we are and who God is, as none of these elements operates independently of the others. Most important, we cannot understand who we are in isolation. We need to understand ourselves in relation to others; here we cannot do without the perspective from people on the margins and the particular pressures they have to endure—pressures that reflect back to us the truth about ourselves.[26] We also need to understand who we are in relation to the God who created us and who transforms us into a new image that we have seen in its fullness only in Jesus Christ, to whom both the Bible and the Christian traditions witness.

More important to the continued reshaping of the church by grace under pressure, however, is the transformation of our images of God. The reference to God can no longer be the ending point of a debate, as is so often the case in our theological discussions. The reference to God cannot be the final trump card of an argument—it must always be the beginning of a new conversation. When we lay our theological cards on the table and invoke images of God, we thereby invite others to do the same and to enter into a process of discernment as to the true nature of God, which requires argument and self-critical reflection informed by the Bible and traditions. In this process, the answers cannot be found in the middle through the lowest common denominator. Answers can be considered genuine (and truly salvific) only if they touch on where the real pain is, where the ultimate pressures of life and death are at stake in our own time, and where the conversation is broad enough to include the margins.

In The United Methodist *Book of Discipline*, the theological task is defined as reflection "upon God's gracious action in our lives," giving "expression to the mysterious reality of God's presence, peace, and power in the world."[27] To find out what God is doing, we need to push beyond the mainline. Those who seek to maintain their mainline positions always run the risk of identifying God with the status quo, and of fashioning God in their own image—which only amounts to yet another special-interest theology.[28] If grace is most active under pressure, we can no longer afford to do special-interest theology for those who have made it, and who are by and large exempt from the more atrocious forms of pressure, pain, and suffering that affect the rest of the world. Confronted with the fact that more than thirty thousand children die every day from hunger and other preventable causes,[29] for instance, we can no longer treat the death of a child, even in our own congregations, as an exception to the rule—as merely another opportunity for counseling designed to integrate the affected parents back into the mainline. We need to ask the hard questions raised by all of those pressured by the deaths of children: where is God in all of this? By the same token, faced with the pressures of enormous and growing economic inequalities, we can no longer treat people suffering from economic pressures as exceptions to the rule. Rather than treating them as candidates for the sort of charity that merely integrates them back into the status quo, we need to ask the hard questions: Where is God graciously at work in this situation? and, what difference does God make? Grace is real only if it manages to prove itself under pressure.

In this way, dealing with the deeper pressures of life challenges the mainline's almost unshakable confidence that it operates in accordance with God. The trust that God is somehow in the middle, the ultimate arbiter of the disagreements of those in charge, shatters when we find God at work where we least expected it, providing grace under pressure. What else would be able to save those forced to endure the greatest pressures in our time, and what else would save those of us from ourselves who are used to exerting pressure?

| Chapter 2 |

Means of Grace under Pressure

YEARS AGO A STUDY ON JOHN WESLEY AND THE SACRAMENTS concluded that modern Methodism has "little spiritual power and very limited intercourse with God."[1] Some people would still agree with this assessment today. Others, however, would contend that our main problem may not be lack of spiritual power but how little difference the church makes in the world.

To the casual observer, it may seem as if these were the only two options available in the church today: On the one side are those who focus on what Christians can do for others—orthopraxis, right action, typically seen as the hallmark of liberal positions. On the other side are those who focus on things they consider spiritual, often emphasizing orthodoxy—right Christian belief, typically seen as the hallmark of conservative positions. The problem with these positions, apart from mindlessly reproducing the long-standing culture wars in the United States, is that both are in danger of becoming self-referential. In the liberal approach, God is often too quickly defined by the benevolent activism of church people, usually white, middle-class, and "first world," who insist on taking things into their own hands; in the process they tend to turn the things they touch into their own image. Here neither God nor the neighbor can be fully seen for what God or the neighbor is. The conservative camps, on the other hand, often forget that even their most sincere efforts of relating to God in spirituality and creed easily become distorted if they are not connected in some ways to learning how to build deeper relationships with their neighbors: to paraphrase 1 John 4:20, how can we relate to God whom we have not seen if we are unable to relate to our neighbors, whom we have seen?

Ironically, both approaches end up losing what they are most concerned about; both the relation to God and the relation to the neighbor suffer. In this chapter, we will push beyond this dichotomy, which has been characteristic of mainline Protestantism for almost two centuries. I will investigate new ways of connecting the spiritual and practical quests in light of alternative ways of relating to God and neighbor. The Wesleyan understanding of the means of grace—which has often been a pawn in the struggle of the two dominant camps—is at the basis of my argument.

The Means of Grace

That the means of grace may be the key to resolving one of the fundamental impasses in the life of the church might come as a surprise. Yet that is not all: I will argue that the means of grace as amended by the Methodist traditions provide the way forward for Christianity as a whole in a world that suffers from deep rifts and pressures. If Methodism has something distinct to contribute to Christianity as a whole—a debate that is far from settled—its reappropriation of the classical means-of-grace tradition might be it.

Keeping with his Anglican tradition, John Wesley defined means of grace as "outward signs, words, or actions ordained of God, and appointed for this end—to be the *ordinary* channels whereby he might convey to men preventing, justifying, or sanctifying grace"[2] (emphasis added). His initial list of the means of grace comprised three elements: "prayer, whether in secret or with the great congregation; searching the Scriptures (which implies reading, hearing, and meditating thereon) and receiving the Lord's Supper."[3] Later he added fasting and Christian conference.[4]

On the backdrop of this list we see again contours of the two dominant camps in the mainline church, the liberal and the conservative. On the one hand, there are those who see the whole purpose of the Christian life in terms of this list of the means of grace, or at least in terms of some of its elements. In the fundamentalist climate of the "Bible Belt," Scripture is still the focal point for conservatives; there are other conservatives who focus more on the sacraments, and yet others who concentrate on a personal relationship to God expressed in prayer and spirituality. On the other hand, liberal Christians cannot help but feel that they should look elsewhere for what really matters in today's church and world. This is related to a basic problem in Wesley's own time, and Wesley was not happy with either side.[5] So far the issue is clear, and this is as far as Methodist theologians have usually considered it.[6] Our task is to find a more constructive way of dealing with the issues at hand. The future of Christianity cannot be entrusted to the narrow confines of the culture wars of the mainline, between liberals and conservatives.

Expanding the Means-of-Grace Tradition

Expanding our vision, we find a first clue in a central element of many of Wesley's writings: his focus on Christian love of God and love of neighbor, sparked by God's own love in Christ.[7] It is this central element of his theology that eventually led him to a radical expansion of his definition of the means of grace. While Christian love of God and neighbor is commonly affirmed in the Wesleyan traditions, Wesley's radical expansion of the means of grace is hardly acknowledged. Yet, as I will show, everything depends on it.

In a later sermon titled "On Zeal," Wesley located the means of grace in a larger framework, unfolding the double focus of his theology in terms of the means of grace. What is perhaps most surprising here is how seriously Wesley took the love of neighbor, which is often treated as an afterthought by the church—as a second step, after the love of God has been declared and celebrated in worship settings. Wesley radically revised this order when he explicitly included what he called "works of mercy"—traditionally understood as good deeds for the benefit of the neighbor—into the list of the means of grace. Here we have one of the most distinctive marks of his theology; Wesley noted that he was fully aware that "this is not commonly adverted to."[8]

This was an extraordinary step for a theologian who did not normally step outside of the boundaries of what was "commonly adverted to," and it therefore needs to be acknowledged as such. More important, however, this late theological insight of Wesley's appears to be in line with the deeper logic at the heart of the Methodist movement and can thus be considered as a summary by the older Wesley of an important element that was present from the beginning without having received explicit reflection.

Developing a vision of what really matters in the Christian life, Wesley worked out a framework of four concentric circles to explicate his point. At the center of these circles is love, more precisely the double focus of love of God and love of neighbor. In the circle closest to the center Wesley located what he called "holy tempers."[9] The next circle is constituted by what he called works of mercy, the third circle by works of piety (which are the traditional means of grace listed above). Only in the outermost circle did Wesley locate the church.

The most remarkable thing about this framework, of course, is the place of works of mercy in relation to works of piety—a fact which some of Wesley's interpreters have noted correctly but not developed further. In agreement with both the prophet Hosea and the evangelist Matthew, Wesley pointed out that "God will have mercy and not sacrifice" (see Hos. 6:6; Matt. 9:13; 12:7). Whenever works of mercy interfere with works of piety, he concluded, the former "are to be preferred." Wesley explained to the surprised readers— mainline Christians, to be sure, including the Anglicans of his day and the Methodists of today—that "even reading, hearing, prayer, are to be omitted, or to be postponed, 'at charity's almighty call'—when we are called to relieve the distress of our neighbour, whether in body or soul."[10]

Before taking a closer look at what is at stake here, let us note that this same pattern can be found as part of the Doctrinal Standards of contemporary United Methodism, in the General Rules. The General Rules start with the concern for doing no harm and doing good—mirroring what Wesley called the works of mercy and spelling out what he had in mind under this rubric—and only then move on to call for the attendance "upon all the ordinances of God"— listing the so-called works of piety.[11] One example of how Wesley's concern for works of mercy pushes far beyond common Christian notions of charity in this context is his rejection of collecting "unlawful interest"; in this way, Wesley directly challenged the economic structures that kept and continue to keep the lower classes in their place, and that, when challenged, might open the doors for alternative ways of life.[12]

While no one would disagree that works of mercy are important in the Wesleyan traditions, we must now try to understand to what purpose Wesley included them into the means-of-grace tradition. In this new model, works of mercy are more than correct actions, or orthopraxis. As real means of grace they must now be understood as channels of God's grace, which convey grace not only to the one who is the recipient of works of mercy but also to the one who acts in merciful ways. A work of mercy can therefore no longer be considered to be a charitable one-way street, leading from the well-meaning Christian to the other under pressure and at the margins. Something comes back in return, which transforms the doer of mercy as well. In doing works of mercy—and this is absolutely crucial—a real encounter with God takes place, which is closely linked to the encounter with the other.

A fresh reflection on works of mercy as means of grace might help us in leaving the old impasse to which the conventional opposition of orthodoxy (right belief) and orthopraxis ("politically correct" right praxis) has led us. Bringing together both works of piety and works of mercy as means of grace, Wesley keeps together the love of the (divine) Other and the (human) other in a special way that merits our attention. Here we encounter a fundamental challenge not only to Methodism but also to contemporary Christianity as a whole. Can the fact that the relation to the divine Other cannot be separated from the relation to the human other help to overcome one of the most detrimental and paralyzing impasses in the church today?

Pursuing further the lines of Wesley's argument, we must now consider the full impact of this challenge. It has been argued, for instance, that works of mercy are means of grace that point to God's presence but not to God's identity. In this model, God's identity would be defined solely by the works of piety.[13] But why would God's identity not also be at stake in the works of mercy? Can anyone have an encounter with God's presence without receiving a glimpse of God's identity? Encountering God's presence in the face of the other somehow also points us to God's identity. We need to see the relation of works of piety and works of mercy in more constructive ways.

Between the Other and the other*

It is not necessary to go to great lengths about the platitude that both works of piety and works of mercy are important. Nobody would disagree with

---

*Lowercase intended

that. The challenge before us is more specific: what does it really mean for Christianity when we begin to understand works of mercy as means of grace? To be sure, this insight merely helps us to catch up with a bigger reality that we do not have to create: whether Christians realize it or not, works of mercy have always been means of grace. The real problem is that Christianity by and large has failed to understand this; and here is a major blind spot not only of those who favor orthodoxy but of those who favor orthopraxis as well.

The problem has two distinct aspects. First, there is a one-sided concern for works of piety and orthodoxy that denies to works of mercy their status as part of the means of grace and considers them as secondary calls to social engagement. Second, a one-sided concern for the works of mercy often forgets precisely the same thing, namely, that works of mercy are not merely good deeds but real means of grace. This twofold problem leads to a common distortion: works of mercy quickly degenerate into acts of charity that are mostly one-way streets; works of piety are pulled into this degenerative process as well, so that they become ineffective and irrelevant.

Let us take a look at the second problem first. If works of mercy are not seen as real means of grace, then we quickly get stuck in the one-way street of charity. In this case, works of mercy might take the shape of good deeds or "outreach" projects, for instance, whereby Christians are acting charitably and do good things for others. But even if those works and actions are done out of love for the neighbor, it is hard to avoid a certain condescending attitude. In this case, the fate of the other under pressure and at the margins is placed in the hands of the one who is acting in a merciful way. It is less clear that the encounter with people at the margins might have a powerful impact on the doer of mercy that goes far beyond the often-reported "feeling good about oneself" when doing things for others.

This is still one of the major blind spots of many Christians who honestly seek to help others at the margins. Not only charitable projects but also social action programs and efforts at advocacy are affected by this problem. During the days of the civil rights movement, for instance, some well-meaning white Americans ended up turning their backs on the African American struggle when they failed to realize that their own liberation was also at stake. Focusing exclusively on what one can do for others is not only incomplete; it is problematic, as any contributions those others might make in return are overlooked. Worst of all, the inability to take others seriously, both in their difference from us and in the contributions they might make to the common cause, results in efforts to mold them into our own image.

This attitude has had detrimental consequences for those who were supposed to be the recipients of works of mercy or the beneficiaries of mainline social activism and advocacy. Native American scholar George Tinker tells the "history of good intentions" of the missions to Native Americans. The missionaries facilitated exploitation, despite their moral integrity and the fact that they did not benefit from exploitation themselves. Tinker traces this phenomenon back to an unconscious attitude of condescension, tied to the idealization of the missionaries' own white culture. At the root of the problem is the inability to enter into relationship and to learn from others—the problem of the one-way street.[14]

In regard to the more recent context, Robert Allen Warrior, another Native American scholar, identifies the problem in a situation where "liberals and conservatives alike" have decided to come to the rescue of Native Americans. The problem has to do with the fact that they are "always using their [own] methods, their ideas, and their programs."[15] Warrior sees hope only if Christians would begin to listen more carefully to others, thus putting an end to what we have identified as the one-way street mentality of many conventional charitable and even social efforts.

Furthermore, where orthopraxis has become a one-way street, both the relation to other people and to God suffers. It is this problem that the orthodox critics may have sensed, but have never quite been able to express in this way. While it is not true that the liberal approaches have intentionally neglected God, as many conservatives charge, the patronizing tendency in which the socially active self approaches the other at the margins tends to be reproduced in relation to God. The focus on orthopraxis is thus related to a concern for the self's reach for God, rather than on God's reach for the self. There is a very real danger in this approach that God becomes an extension of the well-meaning Christian.

In this context, understanding works of mercy as means of grace makes all the difference. If works of mercy are a means of grace, the one-way streets of liberal charity or social activism open up into two-way streets. This changes everything. Works of mercy are no longer about charity or social action, done by some on behalf of others. Rather, works of mercy seek to promote relationships of solidarity, where the unilateral flow of power from the top down is challenged and where *all* are recipients of God's grace. If by acting mercifully Christians are first of all recipients of the grace of God, then the whole concept of social action and of orthopraxis changes. Social action is no longer about what the Reformers called "works' righteousness"—an effort to earn God's grace through good deeds. Just the opposite: social action means placing oneself on the receiving end and being transformed in encounters with other people. In this connection, a renewed relationship to other persons that challenges the unilateral flow of power from the top down—that is, from the established self to the other in need—can contribute to a renewed relationship to the divine Other as well. Liberated from presenting ourselves as the norm and from having to shape others in our own image, we are finally freed to open up to the transforming power of God's grace.

This account helps to understand better what is actually experienced by mainline Christians of all walks of life who have on occasions been forced out of their personal safety zones in the encounter with others. Some people in our churches have undergone real transformation when they began to engage their neighbors in new ways, whether on mission trips to other countries or in places of pressure and need close to home. This is an example of how our praxis tends to precede our theology. Unfortunately—and this is the problem this book and much of my work seeks to redress—the leaders of the church often lack the theological tools to deal with these experiences in deeper fashion. Here is a real problem in the contemporary church that—due both to a dearth of deeper relations to others and to an inability to reflect theologically on these matters— is unable to lead people to the next steps.

The earlier set of problems—a one-sided concern for works of piety that forgets that works of mercy are means of grace—is perhaps more difficult to analyze. Wesley was quite concerned about this, and he warned that Christians had fallen from grace simply because they did not pay attention to the works of mercy.[16] Imagine what this means: good church people who go to church every Sunday, receive Holy Communion as often as possible, pray regularly, and read the Bible every day can fall from grace because they miss something essential of which they are not even aware, namely, the works of mercy as means of grace. This implies that works of mercy are more than what has sometimes been classified the "prudential means of grace," the sort of things that are useful but not required. Following Wesley, we must treat works of mercy as essential means of grace, as neglect of works of mercy destroys Christianity and the church.[17]

No doubt, an exclusive focus on the works of piety, including prayer, reading the Scripture, and Holy Communion, is not enough. But what precisely is the problem? At first sight it looks as if conservative Christians concerned with works of piety would know what liberal Christians concerned with works of mercy sometimes forget, namely, that Christianity is not a set of one-way streets, moving from ourselves to the other and from ourselves to God. For those who understand the thrust of the works of piety in terms of the classical means-of-grace tradition, the focus is reversed. The divine-human relationship is not initiated by humanity, leading to God. Rather, the relationship is initiated by God and thus runs from God to humanity. So why not just expand this position by adding some works of mercy on top of works of piety?

The real problems, however, cut deeper. The focus on works of piety often covers up yet another set of blind spots. This can occur when means of grace are mistaken for the thing itself. One example evident in many conservative Protestant circles is the very common confusion of the Bible as the word of God with the Word of God. If the Bible is a means of grace, then it is indeed a *means* of God's speech—a channel through which God speaks—but it is not automatically identical with it. Wesley addressed the underlying theological problem in his sermon on the means of grace; his meaning has been picked up faithfully by his interpreters.[18]

But even when this confusion is cleared up, serious problems remain. The exclusive focus on the works of piety as means of grace also leads to a common neglect of a concern for other persons in need—a concern of supreme significance to Christianity because it is God's own concern. In our focusing exclusively on God's relation to humanity through the works of piety, God's concern for others is lost and thus the means of grace are defined too narrowly. This narrowness cannot be remedied by simply adding works of mercy on top of works of piety; if works of mercy are truly means of grace, we need to account for their interrelation with the other means of grace. Otherwise, works of mercy become mechanical actions, mere "applications" of a more important set of truths.[19]

There is one more problem, often overlooked, that is perhaps the most troubling one in this connection. Where the relation to the others is not taken into account as a means of grace, the traditional means of grace—reading the Bible, participating in Holy Communion, and praying—are easily distorted. Even the theologically correct concern for moving from God to us, rather than the other way around, can be appropriated in such a way that God's grace becomes self-serving once again; what happens, for instance, when the faithful perform works of piety because they mostly care about themselves and their own salvation? In this case it is hard to see how works of piety could be channels of God's grace in such a way that God can break through to us. As a result the Christian self fails to experience transformation, and the works of piety have lost their challenge. Adding works of mercy on top of works of piety does not, therefore, lead automatically to the quantum leap we are looking for.

In these ways, liberals and conservatives alike end up missing the love of both the human other and the divine Other. Even the conservative concern for God's relation to us in the works of piety is in constant danger of covering up Christian self-interest in the name of God. If the relation to the other person is lost from sight, there is no double check of our relation to the divine Other, as already the writer of 1 John knew: "Those who say, 'I love God,' and hate their brothers or sisters, are liars; for those who do not love a brother or sister whom they have seen, cannot love God whom they have not seen" (4:20). The concern for God does not automatically overcome the self-centeredness of theology. We must ask ourselves: how might even the concern for God's sovereignty be misused to cover up that self-centeredness that is so typical of contemporary "first world" Christianity?

On the other hand, the concern of liberal Christianity, even if pursued with the purest of intentions, is in danger of reinforcing a form of self-centeredness that is unable to find anything in others but its own mirror image. No wonder it fails to find God! In this context, the question becomes, how might the other become a channel of God's grace that helps us to better understand who God is and who we are? Those who take this approach will find it necessary also to pose self-critical questions, such as, who put the other in this place? Thus recognizing their own complicity, they are, for the first time, in a position where they can become aware of their own need for God's liberating and transforming power.

Beyond Orthodoxy and Orthopraxis

The Wesleyan expansion of the means-of-grace tradition pushes beyond the conservative/orthodox and the liberal/orthopraxis camps. In one of his sermons on Jesus' Sermon on the Mount, Wesley made it clear that orthodoxy is not sufficient: "Whatever creeds we may rehearse; whatever professions of faith we make; whatever number of prayers we may repeat, whatever thanksgivings we read or say to God," we may still miss the mark. Yet, Wesley reminds us, the same is true for those in the orthopraxis camp, who merely seek to follow the first two General Rules of doing no harm and doing good without concern for the works of piety.[20]

Nevertheless, this is another conundrum that cannot be resolved by trying to have it both ways—a move that is typical for mainline Christianity. Although Outler noted correctly that Wesley was not interested in playing works of piety and works of mercy against each other,[21] this does not mean that Wesley would be content with the typical harmless bifurcation that affirms both elements but ultimately leaves them unrelated and therefore unchanged. Wesleyan spirituality, as I will show next, puts orthodoxy and orthopraxis in a constructive relationship that transforms both elements.

First of all, relating works of piety and works of mercy challenges and transforms the orthodox and high-church traditions. Traditional Anglican theology does not include the works of mercy in the means-of-grace tradition in the same way that Wesley does. Following in the tradition of Wesley, we need to explore how faithful Christian praxis (which is geared toward solidarity with people in need) helps to reshape matters of piety and doctrine. Outler's helpful point that Wesley was a "folk theologian"[22] can now be understood in a more fundamental sense. It is usually assumed that, as a folk theologian, Wesley was mainly concerned with transmitting a predetermined system of the Christian faith to common people. But in taking seriously works of mercy as means of grace, he also developed some rudimentary theological tools that (even if only in preliminary form) allowed him to listen to and learn from the people. As a result, Wesley's emphasis on the relation of works of piety and works of mercy aims at reconstructing both works of piety and works of mercy.

The genius of Wesley's Methodist approach, and this is my second point, also transforms the concern for right action. Including the works of mercy into the means of grace is a radical challenge for all Christians—those who are not concerned about right action and especially for those who *are*. Works of mercy, as we have seen, can no longer be understood as one-way streets. Combined with the works of piety, they invite an encounter with God, which offers a substantial reconstruction of the modern liberal self and its tendency to shape others in its image, which is due to its social privilege. This presents a challenge to many of the so-called contextual theologies. The theological task is not to adapt Christianity to one's own context, but to transform our contexts in ways that take more seriously both the human other and the divine Other. The so-called works of piety help to guide works of mercy and social action in the search for those contexts where God's saving presence is most needed today.[23]

One example for how works of mercy and works of piety come together is Holy Communion. We must realize that the Christ whom we meet at the Communion table and in the liturgy of the church cannot be another Christ than the one we meet in other persons—especially the marginalized. Holy Communion is communion with Christ who is both "sitting at the right hand of God" (as we confess in the Apostles' Creed) and at work in relations of solidarity with the "least of these" (Matt. 25:40). Holy Communion is therefore no longer merely a private transaction between God and the churched. Holy Communion includes God's concern for all of creation, especially for those who are under pressure and at the margins. The act of eating and drinking together with them at the Eucharistic table is both symbolic and a witness to real solidarity that takes the material world seriously.[24]

One of the most important tasks of theology today is to give an account of how both elements—works of mercy and works of piety—reconstruct themselves whenever they are brought into a dialogue. If works of mercy are introduced into the means-of-grace tradition, a new dynamic is created that affects the works of piety: the Bible is read with new eyes; prayer can no longer be a self-centered enterprise; and Holy Communion opens up to include the "least of these." Likewise, the works of mercy are guided and sharpened by reading the Bible, prayer, and practicing Communion. This may well be the most distinct and constructive contribution of Methodism to the future of theology and the church, with tremendous implications for the world.

Ultimately both works of mercy and works of piety must be reconstructed in light of God's own praxis. Wesley seems to have sensed this in his call for a "religion that is spirit and life; the dwelling in God and God in thee."[25] This is the true importance of the means of grace. The key to understanding those means is not primarily the concern for right doctrine or right action. The means of grace are a central place for experiencing God's gracious presence in specific locations with those who are marginalized and experience the most severe pressures in life.

God's gracious presence, experienced through the various means of grace, is the context in which both orthodoxy and orthopraxis come together. Christian doctrine and Christian praxis are related in the experience of God's presence. Here we are at the very heart of Wesleyan theology and doctrine.[26] Theology—no longer being either a catalog of doctrines subsequently applied to ethics or exclusively preoccupied with questions of action and praxis—can then properly be understood as reflection on praxis. And praxis here means God's praxis in relation to our own. In this way theology and the church can be renewed and transformed creatively.

The Two Poles of the Christian Life

Love of God and love of neighbor were related for Wesley. Wesley's interpretation of the gospel warning not to "lay up treasures upon the earth" is a good illustration, for it points us to what really matters. While the love of God was absolutely central for Wesley, when he encouraged "laying up treasures in heaven," he did not first of all talk about the utterly transcendent; Wesley did not waste any time with theological speculation but pointed to the marginalized neighbor in need.[27] If this were simply good moral advice, we could move on. But here we are back where we started—with the connection between the human other and the divine Other. The concern for laying up treasures with the heavenly Other makes sense only if it is tied to the human other.

Doing works of mercy, laying up treasures in heaven, or whatever other expressions Wesley used were aimed specifically at those at the margins.[28] In his own way, Wesley arrived at what liberation theologians later would call a "preferential option for the poor," taking seriously Matthew 25 and other biblical passages.[29] In recent scholarship there is broad agreement that for Wesley the poor "are at the heart of the evangel and that life with the poor is constitutive of Christian discipleship."[30] We are now clearer about the theological connections: any option for the poor must first of all be God's own option for the poor.

Wesleyan theology thus deals with two poles—God and the poor, that is, people in situations of marginalization and pressure. This is the deeper logic that undergirds the relation of works of piety and works of mercy in terms of the means of grace. In this context, we need to remember that God's presence in Christ is always tied to specific locations. The encounter with those in situations of marginalization and pressure sheds light on our overall understanding of God. If works of mercy are real means of grace, a neat separation of God's presence from God's identity is no longer possible. That is to say, works of mercy—the encounters with the marginalized—are channels of God's grace, which help us understand better both who God is and what God does. While works of mercy do not tell the whole story, they do in fact offer a glimpse of God's identity, as Jesus' own story shows.

We meet God and Christ in the means of grace, which include solidarity with the marginalized through the so-called works of mercy. Here God shows God's face. No method of correlation needs to be implied here; I am not talking about an inherent quality of the marginalized that would point us to God without fault, but about seeking God where God has said God would be. Obviously this is not yet a complete doctrine of God, but our thinking about God can no longer do without this impulse. In this light, the contribution of theologies from the margins can no longer be classified and put aside as "special interest theologies." God's own interest in Christ and the Holy Spirit is at stake. The church must not bypass this fact.

Therefore, Ole E. Borgen's judgment that "modern Methodism" would suffer from "little spiritual power and very limited intercourse with God" is true only if the classic Wesleyan concern for works of mercy and for people under pressure and at the margins is misunderstood as a one-way street. Nevertheless, this comment still serves as a warning not only for Methodists but also for Christianity as a whole, even though the question of the relationship to God has now to be seen in the more specific light of the encounter with those at the margins.

| Chapter 3 |

The Economics of Grace in Global Capitalism

IDEALS OF HOLINESS AND SANCTIFICATION, AT THE HEART OF THE Methodist traditions, have often been tied up with appeals to action. On the surface, this makes perfect sense; if holiness and sanctification are to be more than pious ideas, somebody needs to do something. Yet this attitude has often been taken to extremes, and not just in Methodism. I have often heard both Protestant liberals and Roman Catholic conservatives (and many others in between) say, "God has no other hands than our hands, and no other feet than our feet." What happens if appeals to action are pushed too far?

From the perspective of those who call for action, the most important question is, what can *we* do? Liberation theologies, especially within the context of the so-called first world, have often been misunderstood in this light. Rooted firmly in models of entrepreneurship promoted by capitalism and in Enlightenment ideas of autonomy, "first world" interpreters of liberation theologies could see only an ethical imperative and a call to engage in social activism. A similar fixation on the question, what can we do? is also found in the other, now much more prominent, response to poverty and suffering that promotes acts of charity and social service. A large number of churches, especially in the United States, have caught on to these practices.

There are, however, two major problems with such appeals to action. The first and more familiar one is burnout, or what has also become known as compassion fatigue. How do we keep up long term whatever level of action we choose? This problem has had its own well-known incarnations in earlier decades. But my prediction is that this will soon become a major issue again, particularly as churches are waking up to the fact that there is a whole world beyond their walls. In The United Methodist Church, this welcome awakening is expressed in the modification of its mission statement at General Conference in 2008, from "making disciples of Jesus Christ" to "making disciples of Jesus Christ for the transformation of the world."[1]

The second problem is perhaps more serious but also less obvious in the current climate. How do we prevent our actions and activisms from becoming overbearing and controlling? For the most part, this problem is not even on the map yet, since well-meaning "first world" Christians have little sense that by calling for action and taking things into their own hands they might end up controlling and manipulating those whom they seek to support. In this context, a core problem of the history of nineteenth-century Christian missions repeats itself in a slightly different way: we end up once again shaping other people in our own image—this time, of course, not so much by preaching to them but by trying to be supportive in other ways.

Developing ways to resist these problems is not easy, since they are so ingrained in the culture of our "New World Order" to which both liberals and conservatives subscribe in their own ways. In this chapter, I suggest forms of theological resistance that are once again rooted in the notion of grace. The theological notion of grace provides us with alternatives to both burnout and a mentality of control and pushes us toward a whole new way of life that amounts to nothing less than what in the Christian tradition has been called a "new creation."

A Free-Market Economics of Grace

It is tempting to contrast the free-market economy with what might be called "an economy of grace." At first sight the free-market economy runs on the basis of action and works. Only those who work hard will succeed—or so the story goes. Conversely, an economy of grace runs on the basis of God's free gift. Here, only the recipients of God's gifts will succeed. But at a time in which late, neoliberal, and globalizing capitalism is expanding its reach into every nook and cranny of our lives,[2] both models are easily pulled in by the powers that be.

The first position, the works' righteousness of the free-market economy, can quickly be exposed as an illusion. There are now lots of people, even within the countries of the so-called "first world," who work extremely hard, frequently several jobs at once, who do not succeed.[3] And as to those who succeed: could anyone seriously claim that, seeing as how the average CEO in the United States makes between four hundred and five hundred times the salary of the average worker, some people can indeed work hundreds of times harder than others? This does not even consider the fact that the top twenty private-equity and hedge-fund managers in the United States earn more than twenty thousand times the salary of the average worker.[4] That sort of works' righteousness comes with its own Pelagian doctrine of grace: God gives us the ability to perform well (we tend to tell our children that they can be anything they want to be), but will and action are ours;[5] or, as the motto of the Nike Corporation demands: "Just do it." But the tremendous differences between the wealthiest members of society and the rest—even between different groups within the context of the wealthier countries, let alone between the wealthier countries and the poorer countries around the globe—can hardly be explained that way. How much more will and action can a CEO of a global corporation or a top investor muster compared to a worker in a factory in a country of the "two-thirds world," considering that their incomes may differ by a factor of several hundred thousand times or more?

But what about the second position, the economy of grace? What is wrong with it? First of all, we need to remind ourselves that the global free-market economy is no longer based on works' righteousness alone. Its real success lies elsewhere. Works' righteousness—the belief that we are compensated according to the value or intensity of our labor—is now a more or less convenient cover-up, which lets us maintain appearances, keeps up morale at the top, and keeps those on the underside in place. A substantial part of income is now produced no longer by work but by the stock market. The astounding wealth of CEOs, for instance, is produced more and more by their stock options and other bonus and benefit packages that resemble not the model of works' righteousness but the model of "free grace." The whole idea of the 401(k) retirement programs in the United States, designed mainly for the middle class, is based on a similar concept: the market will ensure the necessary surplus so that our relatively modest contributions to these funds let us live happily ever after. Of course, this confidence in the market has now been shaken in the wake of a tremendous economic crash; but hope in the market continues, as some were able to build huge fortunes even in times of economic downturn and the rest of us appear to have no other choice but to hope for the best. The conclusion, therefore, remains the same after the crash as it was before: those who know how to hook up with the benefits of the market will succeed.[6]

Similar attitudes plague our Christian concept of free grace. The Wesleyan model of prevenient, justifying, and sanctifying grace is often seen in the following fashion: those who know how to hook up with its benefits will succeed. In this process, grace becomes a commodity—something that can be owned like private property and that can be used by its owners for their own purposes, in whatever ways they please. There are close connections between the globalizing economy and this particular economy of grace, and it is no mere coincidence that in both cases those who benefit the most from such "free grace" and all the other blessings life has to offer are the members of the middle and upper classes.

These two positions, works' righteousness and an economy of grace that promotes a sense that the best things in life are free to those who know how to position themselves, resonate with the two problems mentioned at the outset: burnout and control. Burnout can be seen in those who drop out of the pressures of successful careers (the semblance of works' righteousness in the professional world) to pursue a more simple life; it can also be seen in Christians who drop out of the pressures of activism, on the assumption that less action will still give them the desired results. A controlling attitude can be seen not only in those who had to work hard for their success but also in those who, having benefited from the abundant free grace of the market, want to pass on some of their blessings— now, of course, with strings attached. Here the wealthy philanthropist and the well-meaning Christian do not differ much: both assume that they possess something that other people need, and both assume that they already know what is best for them.

An Alternative Economics of Grace

The Christian legacy and its hope for a new creation, however, reaches deeper and suggests an entirely new perspective that leads us beyond controlling activism and its corollary, burnout. This new creation is driven by neither orthopraxis (social activism or service) nor orthodoxy (theological knowledge of how to hook up with grace in ways that allow us to exploit it as a commodity), but by a relation to an alternative energy source that creates an alternative economics of grace.[7]

A first step beyond the commodification of grace is to understand that grace is related to a giver who cannot be commodified. This is close to John Wesley's own solution: "Let nothing satisfy thee but the power of godliness, but a religion that is spirit and life; the dwelling in God and God in thee."[8] Instead of speaking about justification or sanctification, we might use the terms *justifying grace* and *sanctifying grace* to point to the fact that the focus is not on us and on our performance, but beyond ourselves. Ultimately, both justification and sanctification are out of our hands; theologically speaking, they are in God's hands. Moreover, we need to remind ourselves that the grace conveyed to us in the processes of justification and sanctification is always tied to our relationship with God. For that reason, grace can never become a commodity, something that we could appropriate and own like private property.

There can be no "spiritual capitalism," therefore, even though John Wesley has often been misunderstood precisely in this way. Such misunderstandings are among the biggest problems of the church today, not only in regard to the promoters of the much-lamented "prosperity gospel," but also in regard to average mainline churches whose church members and leaders (mostly without being aware of it) bring their business logic to church. Yet Wesley's own encouragement to go "from grace to grace" displayed a different logic. His classical advice, to "stir up that spark of grace that is within you, and he will give you more grace,"[9] was not based on an understanding of grace as commodity or private property, but on an understanding of grace as a growing relationship between Christians and God.[10]

In our current situation, where our thinking as a whole is more and more shaped by the logic of free-market capitalism, the future of Christianity, the church, and even the world depends on whether we understand that the notion of grace cannot be commodified. Grace, understood in the relational way I am proposing here, resists the free-market understanding of the abundant return of an investment or the surplus gained by following orthodox economic doctrine. In other words, grace can no longer be seen simply as a matter of receiving free gifts. Of course, in our current economic system, such gifts are given all the time in the form of—often unmerited—bonuses (the severance pay for CEOs commonly covers two or three years of salary, even in cases where CEOs are fired) and overabundant returns on the right kinds of investments even in times of economic crisis. The bubble economies of recent decades have raised our expectations, even though economic options seem to be somewhat more restricted now in the wake of the bear markets at the end of the first decade of the twenty-first century. Yet an alternative notion of grace cannot be based on the logic of the market; it needs to be based on a relationship with God.

The fundamental difference between thinking about grace in terms of a relationship with God and thinking about grace as a commodity is that in this relationship grace cannot be controlled, because God cannot be controlled. God's gift of grace is "free," not in the sense that it is another resource we can exploit if we know the tricks of how to get it (is that not what church attendance often boils down to?),[11] but in the sense that there is simply no way for us to control it. There is not even a *religious* way to control God's grace, as Martin Luther and later John Wesley realized in their own ways. Grace is what happens in our relationship with God—a relationship that is initiated by God and that invites our response. There is no "substance" or "essence" of grace that exists apart from that relationship.[12] In fact, it can be argued that grace is nothing else but the relationship between God and us.

Wesley called into question an understanding of God's gifts in terms of private property. In fact, he even rejected understanding God's gifts as a loan, because this analogy does not put enough emphasis on our ongoing relationship with God. In terms of our overall argument, we could say that even the image of grace as a loan would allow the further commodification of God's gifts. Receiving God's gifts, in Wesley's thinking, has to do with a relationship. Christians are God's stewards, he said, because "we are now indebted to [God] for all we have; but although a debtor is obliged to return what he has received, yet until the time of payment comes he is at liberty to use it as he pleases. It is not so with a steward: he is not at liberty to use what is lodged in his hands as *he* pleases, but as his master pleases."[13] Stewardship is a concept that is much more radical than we expect: it is about a relationship that challenges the notions of ownership on which capitalism is built.

Wesley's thinking was thoroughly relational, rooted in God's own ways of relating to us. The goal illustrates the way: in his sermon "The New Creation," where Wesley (quite untypically) looked far into the future, he concluded that at the end "there will be a deep, an intimate, an uninterrupted union with God; a constant communion with the Father and his Son Jesus Christ, through the

Spirit; a continual enjoyment of the Three-One God, and of all the creatures in him!"[14] Even the new creation is about relationship rather than ownership.

Such relational thinking creates room for what might be called an "alternative economics of grace"; it leads us beyond one of the fundamental problems of burnout, namely, the illusion that we have to take things into our own hands and that we need to be in charge of everything. It also leads us beyond the idea, so common in the sort of mainline Christianity that has developed in a free-market economy, that our knowledge of the right tricks and sources can help us in exploiting "free grace."

Grace and Resistance

There is one more roadblock, however. Even when we stop thinking about grace in terms of a commodifiable substance and, instead, think about it in terms of a relationship with God, how do we make sure that this relationship stays open and alive? How do we resist the temptation to control and manipulate even this ultimate relationship for our own benefit?

One of the biggest problems at present, made worse by the all-pervasive climate of free-market capitalism, is that relationships are of value only when they produce results. No doubt our relationship with God can be pressed into this category as well. "What is in it for me?" is commonly asked even of our most intimate relationships. Relationships are generally considered successful if we manage to shape in our own image those with whom we are in relation, in order to produce some gain for us. Relationships between employers and employees, for instance, are only deemed successful if employers can shape their staff in such a way that they produce what every employer needs and wants: a surplus. That is now frequently also the way many of us look at the rest of the world, including our own family members: how can these relationships produce a surplus for us? For example, how does the success of children in school or sports enhance the social status of their parents? Or how does the economic status of parents enhance the options of their children, both personal and professional? The challenge is, therefore, how we can escape this trap in our relationships with other people. Equally important, how do we make sure that we escape this trap where our relation to God is concerned?

Elsewhere I have argued that the way we relate to other people is indicative of the way we relate to God.[15] If we are unable to respect other people in all of their differences and complexity—and this is one of the basic problems of our age, even for those who mean well and want to help others—we may also be unable to respect God, despite our best intentions and no matter how respectful our theological language, our liturgies, and our worship services appear. At a time when relationships with others are built not on mutual respect but on economic and other gain, our relationship with God is in trouble, too.

In short, we need to give some serious thought to how our relationships with other people shape up in everyday life. In this context, both social service and social activism models may lead us to a first step beyond crude market logic. After all, people who try to help others realize, at least to some degree, that other people matter. But in both models, relationships often get distorted. In trying to help others, are we not too often tempted to shape them in our own image? Social service models, for instance, aim at filling in the gaps that separate others from us, usually taking for granted that our own position is the standard. Social action models, too, often operate as if they know what others really need— a place at our table, for instance, or a lifestyle that resembles ours. If we manage to integrate others into the status quo, and in this way help them to become more like us on the inside, our job is done.

The problem stems from our attempts to build relationships from positions of power and control, that is, from the top down. For example, well-meaning parents tell their children "others are just like us." To be sure, this is an improvement over the sort of attitudes that used to consider others as less than fully human. Nevertheless, by considering others to be just like us, we make ourselves the norm and deal with others on our terms, never able to realize, let alone respect, how others may be different from us and how that difference might be of value.

An understanding of grace in terms of relationship challenges us to build relationships differently. A first step in resisting top-down perspectives is to realize that others are *always already* part of who we are, whether we realize this or not. Our identities are shaped in relation to others, whether positively through the guidance of our parents, teachers, and friends, or negatively through repressions in which we identify ourselves negatively as being unlike poor people, ethnic minorities, or people of other sexual orientations. And sometimes our identities are even shaped on the backs of other people, including those who work for low wages so that we can live more comfortably. Here we need to understand first of all not how "they are like us" but how "we are like them"—that is, what it is that connects us. How did they contribute to shaping our identities? And what else can we learn by seeing ourselves in the mirror of others?

Real relationships will need to take into account the existing mutuality between others and us. This is not always pleasant; sometimes it will require us to face some hard truths about ourselves. But in this context, the other also can make some positive contributions to who we are; this insight leads us to a more fruitful theological question as well: how are we like God? (Think of the *imago Dei* not as what we are now but as what we are to become in relation to God.) Or how might God *reshape* who we are? This is the ultimate question of a theology of grace.

In reshaping our relationships with others, we might have a chance of reshaping our relationship with God also. On these grounds, we can then develop new forms of resistance against the logic of the free-market economy that go directly against those one-sided relationships that constitute the pillars of effective business relations in the current embodiment of free-market economics, where a few benefit at the expense of all others.[16]

Return to the Means of Grace

Wesley's thinking about the means of grace provides additional support for my argument of a parallel between our relationships with God and with other people. As we have seen in the previous chapter, Wesley expanded—and in the process reshaped—the traditional idea of the means of grace, understood as the channels through which we receive God's grace into our lives. Expanding a more traditional list of the means of grace, which included prayer, Bible, and Holy Communion, Wesley added works of mercy. What is more, in cases of conflict he argued that works of mercy were to be preferred. This argument, far from being merely another interesting theological idea, goes deep because it reflects the way in which Wesley pursued his ministry and lived his life.

Once works of mercy are seen as a means of grace, a new way opens up beyond the impasses of current understandings of social activism and social service. The main focus is now no longer on what *we* can do. If everything starts with grace, the question is first of all what *God* can do. Furthermore, the notion of grace itself broadens here. Our understanding of grace becomes even more thoroughly relational. Grace happens in our relation to God and—this is the new challenge of adding works of mercy to the means of grace—in our relation to other people as well, especially to those on the margins and under pressure. The emphasis of these relationships is no longer primarily on what we can do for others and how we can reshape them in such a way that they fit our expectations. The emphasis is now on a new kind of mutual relationship where, in our encounters with others who cannot be controlled (is that not the ultimate challenge that people who are different pose to us—that they have their own ways of resisting our control?), God's grace freely flows into our lives in ways that we cannot control.

This new kind of relationship ceases to work where it is pulled into the expectations of the market. Yet grace based on this alternative form of relationship is no longer a matter of the market, of private property or personal gain, where one party gains at the expense of the other. This form of grace can no longer be used as a commodity. Here, something new happens: new energy is set free that leaves no room for burnout or for the morbid fantasies of control. Was it this that sustained Wesley through all the long years of ministry?

The form of grace under discussion here is no longer a free-for-all—a sort of free-floating energy that can be used for almost any purpose. Grace now has a specific direction. It is tied to the lives of those who are different, those whom we usually do not notice because they inhabit a lower class or because they are born into a race or gender that we consider less prestigious; it opens our eyes for God's own ways of bringing about a new creation in the midst of pain and suffering. Without works of mercy as means of grace—ways of receiving God's grace through relations with others, relations that are no longer understood primarily as social service or activism—we will not know who we are or where to go. No wonder Wesley was concerned that, due to the neglect of works of mercy, some Christians had fallen from grace, despite all their works of piety.[17]

This leads us far beyond the recent dichotomy of "compassionate conservatism" and structural welfare programs. In both cases, it is assumed that the main goal is to integrate people back into the system. In both cases, grace is also tied to the system: grace is whatever helps us to support the status quo and to raise people to the next level within the system (like receiving welfare or winning the lottery). In this context, grace does not present a challenge to, and has no claim on, those within the system (whether liberal or conservative) who seem to "have it all," including the favor of God. Such grace has no direction other than going with the flow. Such grace is manifest in what is often considered to be the true reward and gratification of social service and activism for middle-class people: to feel better about themselves at the end of the day and thus to be enabled to keep things the way they are.

Envisioning works of mercy as being means of grace changes everything. Grace that emerges in new kinds of relationship with God and other people leads to a new perspective. More pointedly, in the context of free-market capitalism, new energy and a new direction emerge precisely where we push beyond commodified notions of grace and controlling relationships with others. This new situation develops where we allow our relations to other people to be reshaped in such a way that they also reshape our relation to God.[18]

New Creation

If grace is what happens in our relationships with God and other people, there is little sense in rehearsing the old question of whether we are talking about an "otherworldly" or a "this-worldly" process. A new perspective emerges, which was also reflected in Wesley's understanding of the doctrine of salvation. In his sermon "The Scripture Way of Salvation" (based on Ephesians 2:8 "ye have been saved"[KJV]), Wesley tells us that salvation is not primarily to be understood as going to heaven or eternal happiness. This message may have been as surprising to mainline Christianity then as it is now. Rather, salvation is what takes place here and now: "ye are saved" or "ye have been saved" is how Wesley translated the passage from Ephesians.[19] This does not mean that the future of salvation does not matter; the point is that there is simply no need to play the "otherworldly" and the "this-worldly" off against each other. Our concern for how we relate to God and to others here and now, and for what God is doing in these relationships, does not diminish our expectations for the future but *focuses* them—in such a way that they shape up as a critique of the powers that be, from which we need to be saved here and now. The problem with the common focus on otherworldly issues is that it too often leaves a vacuum, which the interests of the free-market economy are more than happy to fill.

The goal of it all is nothing less than a new creation. If this creation is real in Jesus Christ and in those who are in Christ (2 Cor. 5:17), then the point is not whether this new creation is transcendent or immanent, futuristic or presentic, but where it is happening now, what it looks like, and how it transforms the real world.[20]

Where does this all lead? Not even the sky is the limit.[21] Directed and empowered by the gracious actions of God in our lives and in the world, Christians have the unique opportunity to resist the powers that be and to build something new. If anything, this is the core insight that connects the various approaches of liberation theology. The categories of social activism and ethics, often introduced to interpret the concerns of liberation theology by well-meaning observers and outside interpreters, can only be misleading in this context.

This new creation, brought about where God's grace is at work, reaches all the way into the one thing that is probably most unthinkable for us at the moment: the transformation of the free-market economy. We have been so conditioned to think "capitalism is here to stay," that we have given up imagining alternatives. But the experience of the alternative economy of God's grace will not let us rest easy even with a supposedly triumphant global capitalism.

God's gracious actions—which reshape the powers that be in relationship with the marginal people of Israel (Israel had always been a small, rather insignificant set of tribes, compared to the powerful nations of its time), the marginal Jesus Christ (operating at the margins of the ancient world and of his own people), and even the marginal Wesley (intentionally operating at the margins of the Church of England and of society)—redirect our current attempts to take things into our own hands. God's alternative economy of grace leads us in new directions and ushers in a new creation that may look quite different from the old.[22]

One all-too-common misunderstanding is that this new creation relates mainly to the notion of sanctifying grace, as the place where people put grace into action and begin taking things into their own hands. But this leads us back into close proximity with the old issues of works' righteousness, burnout, and control of others. A new vision emerges where we rethink this position, beginning with prevenient grace and justifying grace. In prevenient grace, according to Wesley's understanding, we grasp for the first time who we really are before God. Even though this may entail a fairly dim view of things, understanding who we really are before God includes some glimpse into understanding who we really are in relation to our neighbors as well. Justifying grace could be viewed in a similar light: if forgiveness of our sins is to make sense, then it needs to include our relation to both God and our neighbors. In this way, prevenient and justifying grace open the way for a broader vision of sanctifying grace as well: unless we begin to live our lives in mutual and noncontrolling relationships with God and neighbor, the new creation is simply another pious illusion; and we are right back where we started.

| Chapter 4 |

Empire and Grace

Methodism and Empire

CHRISTIANITY WAS BORN IN THE CONTEXT OF THE ROMAN EMPIRE. The temptation to adapt to empire and to become a part of it has accompanied Christianity ever since. After all, Jesus himself was tempted by an imperial mind-set. The temptations he endured, as reported in the Gospels, were the temptations of empire, like the devil's offer of control over all the empires of the world, which Jesus duly declined (Matt. 4:8–10).

If empire poses a challenge for Christianity, how does Methodism fare in the context of empire? Two key problems emerge if we put the question this way. The first problem has to do with the metamorphoses of empire. We are usually able to identify empire in its most blatant forms, such as in the Roman Empire, the Crusades of the medieval empires in Europe, nineteenth-century colonialism, the German Third Reich, and several of the more recent moves of the administration of former United States president George W. Bush. But we find it more difficult to see empire in softer forms of power. What about the United States before and after Bush, for instance? What about the soft colonialisms of earlier times, whose emissaries were supposed to help, educate, train, and support? What about Bartolomé de Las Casas, who defended the humanity of the Amerindians during the early years of the Spanish conquest but kept insisting on their need for cultural and religious improvement?[1]

The second problem has to do with simplistic assumptions about religion and politics and the relation of the two. It is commonly known, for instance, that the Council of Nicaea in 325 CE was called and influenced by the Emperor Constantine. Unfortunately, this issue has usually been addressed by trying to separate religion and politics. Most theologians proceed as if there were a pristine theological core, which remained more or less untouched by the political affairs of empire. Others reject Nicaea altogether, because they note its political nature. The modern conceptual separation of religion and politics has made things worse in this regard. But can we really assume that religion and politics run on different tracks? Were not Constantine's politics undergirded by a robust theology, which clearly identified God at work in favor of the empire?[2] And can an alternative theology even be imagined without alternative political connotations?

John Wesley offered a first clue that helps us address those two problems, when he stated, "Religion must not go from the greatest to the least, or the power would appear to be of men."[3] As I pointed out in chapter 1, this is a remarkable insight on many levels. Yet this insight is of particular importance in light of the two problems noted here, as it illumines the relation of religion and politics, and it helps us get our bearings on empire in both its harder and softer forms.

Let me start with the second problem, the relation of religion and politics. Mainline Christianity has hardly considered the possibility that religion might have a certain directionality. When Wesley talked about religion going from the top down, he commented on religion in relation to power. There is a problem, said Wesley, when religion works hand in glove with top-down power.[4] This poses the question of how Methodism and Methodist theology shape up in light of this problem. If we begin to understand that certain combinations of religion and politics are problematic, what are the alternatives? Some might suggest that we separate religion from politics; but that option does not appear to exist in Wesley's statement. Those on top—the "greatest," who are used to operating from the top down and who know how to make things happen that way—follow a certain logic that also shapes the logic of a certain kind of religion. We might add that even those in the middle and those at the bottom, who look to the top to get things done, become part of this logic.

The alternative would be to reflect on religion as moving from the bottom up, which happened to be the initial direction of the Methodist movement. In the words of John Walch, one of Wesley's most congenial interpreters, Wesley assumed that "all religious movements for reform began among the poor, moving slowly up the social ladder until finally, in the millennial day, they touched the nobility; conversely, skepticism and Deism began among the great and filtered downwards."[5] It should also be noted that Wesley was an outspoken critic of both the Spanish conquest and the emerging British imperialism of his day. For instance, his critique of the slave trade was a critique of the colonial system as a whole, which was based on the exploitation of others in order to accumulate wealth and power.[6] Religion and power are not separated here but put together in a different way. The power of religion these early Methodists saw at work moved from the bottom up—no doubt a surprise to many—thereby raising some interesting theological questions. If, unlike top-down power, this bottom-up power cannot immediately be explained as being "of men," whose power is it?

This view from the underside was so pervasive that it found its way even into the hymns and poetry of the Methodist movement. Unfortunately the following verses of hymns by John Wesley's brother Charles cannot be found in any of the official hymnals of the churches:

> The rich and great in every age
> Conspire to persecute their God,
> Ambitious priests against Him rage,
> And scribes, of empty learning proud,
> They grieve Him by His members' pain,
> And scourge, and crucify again.
>
> We still the old objection hear,
> Have any of the great, or wise,
> The men of name and character
> Believed on Him the vulgar prize?
> Our Saviour, by the rich unknown,
> Is worshipped by the poor alone.
> The poor, we joyfully confess
> His followers and disciples still,
> His friends, and chosen witnesses,
> Who know His name, and do His will,

Who suffer for our Master's cause,
And only glory in His cross.[7]

The strong words of these stanzas cannot be found even in the recently edited volume *Songs for the Poor: Hymns by Charles Wesley.*[8] While the hymns collected in that volume show well the dedication of the Wesleys to the poor, what is missing is a clearer sense of directionality of religion and of the resulting conflicts: taking the side of the poor implied a challenge to the rich and a recognition of the distortions introduced by those who enjoy wealth and privilege.[9]

The Wesleyan sense of the direction of religion also helps us deal with the first problem, the definition of empire. Empire might be understood in very broad terms as this top-down power that is "of men," which has the means to control everything and thus to transform the world in its own image. This top-down power can take many different shapes and forms. It is perhaps most clearly visible in the use of military force; throwing bombs out of airplanes symbolizes a power that moves straight from the top down and that approaches omnipotence the less it has to fear repercussions (following the classical logic of Aristotle's first unmoved mover). But this top-down power might also be embodied in certain humanitarian efforts that seek to bring the perceived benefits and achievements of our lifestyles to others. Teaching others "how to fish" (instead of giving them fish), the paradigm of some much-admired programs, assumes that other people elsewhere are incapable of taking care of their most basic needs such as fishing. Consequently, we need to look for empire, even in "postcolonial" times, when most of the classic colonialisms of the nineteenth and twentieth centuries have been put to rest. Top-down power is a pervasive problem that can take hard or soft forms; we need to address it as *theologians* and as *Christians,* not merely as a political issue. More important, we must confront it as that which shapes our theology and our faith, whether we realize it or not.

In sum, the problem with empire is the sort of top-down power that moves from "the greatest to the least" and that is unable to respect alternative expressions and ways of life. The result is that the expressions of the divine that do not fit with the status quo are not respected, either. The problem with all of this is that our images of God and of God's power are shaped by powers of which much theology and the church are simply unaware. In two recent projects,

I have talked about this as empire, defined as massive concentrations of power that permeate all aspects of life (even the religious ones) and that cannot be controlled by any one actor alone.[10]

A positive project grows out of these observations. If we begin to pay attention to how a theological tradition has been shaped by empire (consciously and unconsciously), we can then take a look at what I have called its "theological surplus,"[11] for example, that which escapes the clutches of empire and points beyond it. This is the good news: empire is not all-powerful, and some developments within Methodism offer proof of this. Empires have never been able to assimilate the divine completely. Sometimes we find the roots of theological surpluses in a basic ambivalence, the existence of which is itself a witness to the limits of empire. Postcolonial theorist Homi Bhabha notes how ambivalence is disturbing to colonial discourse and how it "poses an immanent threat to both 'normalized' knowledges and disciplinary powers."[12] The challenge, he argues, is a "*double* vision, which in disclosing the ambivalence of colonial discourse also disrupts its authority."[13]

Historian David Hempton has found such ambivalence at the heart of the Methodist tradition: "Methodism at its heart and center had always been a profoundly countercultural movement. It drew energy and personal commitment from the dialectics arising from its challenge to accepted norms in religion and society. It thrived on opposition, but it could not long survive equipoise."[14] One of the key insights of Hempton's book *Methodism: Empire of the Spirit* is that Methodism thrived on dialectical tensions, beginning with Wesley himself: "It was Methodism's genius that throughout the English-speaking world it was able to act for so long both as a countercultural movement of populist revivalism and as an enforcer of social stability and sobriety, though not always in the same place at the same time. It was Methodism's misfortune . . . that it could not oscillate between these poles forever."[15] How, then, have the Methodist traditions shaped up in relation to empire, and what difference might they make in the context of empire today?

The Beginnings

Like Christianity, Methodism was born in the context of empire. The British Empire of the days of early Methodism represented a typical colonial power. Yet, like early Christianity, Methodism had a radical edge that could not easily be assimilated by empire: early Methodists were considered to be "disturbers of the world."[16] Whether intentional or not, Methodism had a tendency to get in trouble with traditional authorities, both social and ecclesial.[17] Methodism transgressed established boundaries between clergy and lay, young and old, rich and poor, educated and uneducated. To be sure, the ambivalence that Methodism introduced into the empire's struggle for order and control originated from below. In the words of David Hempton: "This lack of official control was exacerbated by the fact that Methodism often took strongest root in marginal areas, scattered settlements, and new industrial and mining environments where the traditional social cement was weakest."[18] From the beginning, Methodism had deep roots in the worlds of lower-class and marginalized people. In its beginnings in the United States, African Americans who had resisted Christianity for almost a century converted to Methodism after the 1770s.[19]

Even historian E. P. Thompson, who has otherwise identified Methodism as a "religion for the poor" rather than "of the poor," acknowledges a counter-cultural spirit in early Methodism.[20] In tension with Wesley's more authoritarian style, Methodism included democratic elements, due not only to its lay preachers, but also to forms of self-government within the societies. In Thompson's words: "Wesley could not escape the consequences of his own spiritual egalitarianism. If Christ's poor came to believe that their souls were as good as aristocratic or bourgeois souls then it might lead them on to the arguments of the *Rights of Man*."[21] A real alternative to empire emerges here, as this is no empowerment "from above," where power would be given to people by those who are higher up in the system. In early Methodism people were finding their own voice and developed their own resilience to the system.

Hempton, seeking to avoid a narrow interpretation of the Methodist movement in terms of class, has noted that class conflict and religious conflict are always related. His point is well taken that religious movements can be tied to radical change and that social movements are never completely secular.[22] While economic reductionism is not helpful, church people and theologians are more likely to need to be reminded that theological reductionism is not helpful either. Religion never develops in a vacuum, and a decision needs to be made as to whether it pursues the way "from the greatest to the least" or not. It seems that already Wesley was able to learn from the lower classes and that the Methodist movement was able to hold on to a theological surplus and to make a difference precisely for that reason.

Nevertheless, Methodist resistance to empire was not without tensions. Thompson has stood for others when noting the traits of Methodism that made it fit for empire. The Methodist work discipline, for instance, could easily lead to psychic exploitation. Moreover, Methodism, while supporting workers at times, also contributed to the ideology of the Industrial Revolution.[23] Tensions have also been portrayed by Gregory Schneider, who has noted the domestication of the Methodist impulse: "If it gave common people the opportunity to establish their own religious life, to think and act for themselves, it also catered to their need for charismatic and authoritarian 'fathers' who would perpetuate dependence in their spiritual 'children' and a nondemocratic ethos in what they called the 'family of God.'" Schneider continues, "[T]he public, political significance of Methodism must be seen in similarly ambiguous terms."[24] Yet Schneider's conclusion—that "the history of Methodist evangelicalism does not lend itself easily to any moral or political agenda, be it progressive or conservative"[25]—does not necessarily follow. There is a sort of ambivalence that leads to an adjustment to the status quo, but there is also a sort of ambivalence that points toward resistance.

When all is said and done, the fact that Methodism helped people to find their own voice and power, inside and outside the church, is significant. The so-called priesthood of all believers, a term that had been around since the Reformation, helped unsettle the status quo both in the church and in the world.[26] A "theological surplus" can be found where laypeople engage in ecclesial functions once thought appropriate only for the clergy, such as preaching and holding church office. This story is by no means limited to the Methodism of the eighteenth century. My mother, coming to Methodism in Germany from the Lutheran Church in the 1960s, still experienced this empowerment: in a situation where there was little opportunity for laypersons, and for women in particular, the opportunity to assume positions of leadership in the Methodist communities made a real difference. It is not surprising, therefore, that Methodism was received especially well "in areas least amenable to paternalistic influence," as Hempton has pointed out.[27]

In these developments, the matter of intent is a secondary issue. While Wesley's educational work, for instance, may not have had an explicitly subversive intent, as Ken Bedell has argued, the question is how it functioned in the context of empire in which it found itself.[28] This emphasis on education took on a clearly subversive shape in Primitive Methodism. In their Sunday schools, the so-called Primitive Methodists taught children not only to read (a move that was generally accepted as appropriate since it helped them to read the Bible), but also writing and math in order to gain valuable skills, a praxis that was not endorsed by mainline Methodism.[29]

Unlike in Britain, the beginnings of Methodism in the United States are located in a postcolonial situation.[30] The United States won their independence from Britain shortly before Methodism organized itself in 1784. As the subsequent success stories of both Methodism and capitalism in the United States indicate, both seem to thrive in postcolonial situations. From the United States, Methodism spread around the world in the wake of postcolonial expansions, adapting to the needs of new situations.

In this context, Methodism accommodated to newly emerging imperial interests in ways that turned on their head the anti-imperial traits of early Methodism. Its shifting attitudes toward slavery in the United States are telling: while it opposed slavery early on, Methodism later endorsed it. When the Monroe Doctrine was put forth in 1823, which declared the United States' interests in Latin America, Methodism was quick to respond by setting up schools and other initiatives.[31] When the idea of Manifest Destiny was formulated in the middle of the nineteenth century, proclaiming that it was the God-given destiny of the United States to expand all the way to the Pacific Ocean, Methodism did not stand up in protest but expanded with the country. Under the conditions of what I have called a "postcolonial empire,"[32] the lack of a response is often sufficient to comply with the dynamics of empire. In situations of substantial power differentials it is not necessary to promote empire actively—not resisting the flow of empire is enough. Any theological surplus will have to be identified between the lines, therefore, following the sort of ambivalence that is produced from below, for instance in African American Methodism and in other places at the margins.

In sum, despite its location in the context of two empires—the British and the American—Methodism and its theology maintained a spirit of resistance.

As Methodism became more established, this spirit of resistance was increasingly subjected to the pressures and temptations of the status quo, but it never faded completely. As religion refuses to go "from the greatest to the least," a theological surplus emerges that is worth being investigated. If it made a difference in its own time, it may still inspire us to make a difference today.

The Nineteenth and Twentieth Centuries

As we have seen so far, empire was not able to take over early Methodism completely. To understand the difference Methodism made in the past—and that it might still make today—we need to investigate this ongoing relation of Methodism and empire. The nineteenth and twentieth centuries merit somewhat closer scrutiny in this regard because they contain many of the seeds of the current situation. A closer look at Methodism in the United States is warranted, because here Methodism thrived during a longer period than anywhere else.

The first half of the nineteenth century was a time of great energy. The laity was a driving force: Methodism's initial spread around the world was organized and carried out by laypeople, rather than by clergy. The following observation by Hempton sets the stage: "Methodism, like Pentecostalism, was a cultural revolution from below, not a political or ecclesiastical program imposed from above. It grew without external sponsorship and thrived among youthful and mobile populations exploiting the opportunities of new global markets."[33] Perhaps not surprisingly, women made up the majority of members. In all of these developments, however, empire was never far: "From the British side Methodism followed the trade routes and military deployments of early imperialism . . . From the American side the push westward to the Pacific Ocean was equally relentless and inexorable."[34] This does not necessarily mean that Methodists were intentionally endorsing imperialism or that they always benefited from it. There is no reason to doubt that Methodists meant well and were intent on making a positive difference, even though the outcomes could be quite troublesome.

Here is another example of the ambivalence of Methodism under the conditions of empire, an ambivalence that can produce not only resistance but also adaptation. Methodism did indeed thrive "on the margins and frontiers of race and class, continental expansion and empire." While resistance was part of these tensions, Hempton makes us aware of another trajectory as well: "Everywhere, Methodists began as cultural outsiders, but through work discipline and unquenchable passion for education, they remorselessly moved to the cultural center, sometimes with remarkable speed."[35] To be sure, Wesley questioned this sort of success story already in his own times: he sensed that, as the Methodists moved up in social status, they seemed to lose their connection to the heart of the Methodist project. His premonition was correct, because this was often precisely what happened throughout the history of Methodism. In the United States, for instance, slavery was first renounced and later affirmed; women were first liberated and later subdued. In post-Wesleyan England, as conflicts erupted along the lines of class, radicals were expelled and traditional chapels were built due to the desire for respect and acceptance by the powers that be.[36]

From the nineteenth century on, Methodism was officially recognized as "mainline." By 1850 Methodists made up 34 percent of Christianity in the United States, and money began to flow, changing some of the basic paradigms. New qualities sought in preachers, for instance, were designed to make them more acceptable to the middle class. Among these qualities were education, self-improvement, and a reputation for philanthropy.[37] In this context, dominant culture and religion went increasingly hand in hand. Mission scholar Dana Robert gives one example of this development: "The late nineteenth century women's missionary movement conflated culture with religion, attributing the strengths of western culture to its Christianity, and the weaknesses of non-western culture to other religions."[38]

The theological foundations of these developments lay in a fundamental trust in the perfectibility of humanity, and in so-called providential means, such as the spread of empire and the English language. Also fundamental were the emphasis on personal conversion, the witness of the Spirit, the cultivation of perfect love, and the anticipation of heavenly rewards.[39] These theological foundations pointed to an optimism based on a firm trust in the righteousness of the cause of mainline U.S. Methodism; while it would have been understood that there would always be some shortcomings, it was inconceivable that the situation as a whole might be headed in the wrong direction.

An example of this optimism was the life and work of John R. Mott (1865–1955), a U.S. Methodist layperson and one of the most prominent leaders of the

Protestant missionary and ecumenical movements of his time. His optimism was based on a firm trust in the power of God and the lordship of Christ.[40] Mott harbored no doubt that the success of mainline missions was guided by the divine. In his early book *Strategic Points in the World's Conquest*, he insisted that "God Himself has given all the increase."[41]

Mott's goal was to move Christianity to a position of global dominance; and the "evangelization of the world in this generation" was his project.[42] This could happen, however, only if mainline Christianity was united; and so Mott bridged the gap between various branches of the mainline, such as the social gospel (liberal) and conservative Christianity. In this same spirit, he sought to bring together piety and progress, faith in God's revelation in Christ with faith in the achievements of modern science.[43] Of great help in bridging these gaps was the fact that both liberals and conservatives shared in the basic optimism that marked the age, pulling together Christ and progress. In the words of South African missiologist David Bosch: "Both liberals and conservatives shared the assumption that Christianity was the only basis for a healthy civilization; this was a form of consensus so fundamental that it operated mainly on an unconscious, presuppositional level."[44] While the shared goal of evangelizing the world in this generation was not always clearly defined and debates about the meaning of this task continued, it is not hard to see how a basic theological optimism, combined with a sense of the value of Western civilization and of one's own achievements, would indeed provide strong bonds between various camps. Ambivalence here did not contribute to resistance but came to support the hegemonic project: "Sometimes Mott and his co-workers succeeded in keeping the new and fragile ecumenical boat afloat with the aid of fortuitous or unintentional ambiguities."[45] What was virtually absent was a stance that would have provided a challenge.

Empire lurks in the back of this project, albeit in postcolonial fashion. Bosch describes the situation thus: "The United States was not involved in the scramble for colonies; missions, however, provided Americans with an important 'moral equivalent' for imperialism."[46] Just as the Northern European colonial powers prided themselves in having steered clear of the worst atrocities of the Spanish conquest, so the United States prided itself in having mostly avoided the colonial entanglements of the British and other Northern European nations. U.S. foreign missions could be presented as "national altruism" (Bosch's term[47]), responding to what Mott called "the range and depths of human need, and of the infinite value of Christ's program to meet it."[48]

Most interesting for our overall argument is the fact that mission was less and less seen as a one-way street in this context. Looking at this development in light of the challenges of empire, however, makes us realize some of the deeper problems that can emerge even in this approach, the overall logic of which we endorsed in previous chapters. Here is Hempton's summary of the development of Methodist overseas missions: "On the whole they believed in forming partnerships with local people and not lording over them."[49] Mott's approach clearly followed this commendable pattern. Nevertheless, Mott still identified a top-down structure, which is typical even for many efforts at forming partnerships today: "God has given to some movements a larger and richer experience than others." Mott's narrative began with the United States and then moved on to Britain: "Because of her world-wide empire Great Britain is able . . . to do more for missions than any other land. Fully one third of the non-Christian world is under her own flag, and her political influence is probably greater with another third than is that of any other Protestant power." Germany was next, Mott claimed, since "the German universities are the most influential in the world of thought."[50]

In his later years Mott appeared to be somewhat more enlightened, calling, in 1928, for an end to the distinction between "sending" and "receiving" churches and promoting greater equality and collaboration. Nevertheless, it seems that the younger churches did not quite experience it that way.[51] Mott's idea of collaboration was indeed skewed, when he noted that both the younger and the older churches benefit from collaboration, but that the process begins with the "mission boards of Europe and North America" as they "unite in sending out to the fields which they are serving groups of their most statesmanlike representatives to take counsel with the trusted leaders of the Churches and missions." While Mott rejected "any sense of superiority or inferiority" and affirmed a "full recognition of the varieties of Christian experience" and "a frank admission that no one member of the group possesses all the truth, but that each has some special contribution,"[52] nowhere did he call for the reversal of power structures. Such an embodiment of what we today might call "unity in difference" leaves the conventional power structures intact, despite the most genuinely felt affirmations of partnership.

There is no reason to doubt that Mott's intentions were benevolent and that he took his theological commitments seriously. In all this, he sought not only to follow Christ but also to extend the reach of Christ. Yet his image of Christ as Lord looked suspiciously like the lords of his age, like the top politicians and business leaders with whom Mott was in close relation and who shared and supported his ambitious goals.[53] What was lost was a sense that the lordship of Christ might take alternative shapes that challenge even the most benevolent status quo. While Mott represented the general mood of the age, critical voices were also projected early on. Already in 1898 an article in the *Methodist Review* pointed out the close link between missionary and colonial interests: "There is no chance to shut one's eyes to the relation of missions to the success of governmental colonizing schemes," wrote the author.[54] The quest for a theological surplus spans the history of the church.

There is indeed a theological surplus to be mined here. It can perhaps best be seen in a different area that today escapes the attention of most churches, namely, the world of labor. Clearly, Methodism thrived under the rule of capitalism. There are parallels, for instance, between Methodism and Adam Smith's model of a "religious free market," including its character as a popular religious association, its emphasis on discipline, and the fact that it was financed by voluntary contributions and book sales.[55] Yet capitalism and the Industrial Revolution also created strong tensions, especially for the workforces that ensured its success. Wesley and some of the early Methodists were acutely aware of these problems. Although in the course of the nineteenth century this awareness faded, it was to be recovered at the turn of the twentieth century.

At the end of the nineteenth century, with its global expansions growing ever stronger, Methodism had become mostly middle-class. Religious virtue and economic success were now commonly associated, as were economic failure and immorality. The current phenomenon of the "gospel of prosperity" has deep roots in the logic of this middle-class theology; it is shared by the mainline churches insofar as God is commonly identified at the top and on the side of the successful—a problem that is still not recognized by mainline theology even today. Historian Frederick Norwood put this phenomenon in the strongest words: "In every case the leadership of the local church has been dominated by the managerial class . . . Sometimes the churches have been practically owned by the dominant industrial power."[56] While Norwood's comment addressed the early twentieth century, the parallels to the early twenty-first century cannot easily be dismissed.

Nevertheless, the church did not abandon the workers altogether, and thus preserved the source of another classic Methodist ambivalence that would lead not only to challenges to empire but also to a significant theological surplus. For instance, during the steel strike of 1919 that took place in various U.S. states, the Interchurch World Movement and the Federal Council of Churches set up a commission of inquiry, which reported to President Woodrow Wilson. This commission was chaired by none other than John R. Mott. It documented common abuses of workers, such as twelve-hour workdays, low pay, seven-day weeks, long shifts, and lack of input from workers. In the wake of this new awareness of labor issues, many of these evils were corrected and attitudes of church people toward labor changed.[57] An early speech by Mott, in 1893, captured a potential theological surplus emerging from his focus on Christ: "If Christ were to travel in our country today, he would be concerned about the poor and [in Andrew Carnegie's phrase] could teach the rich the true 'gospel of wealth.'"[58] Mott's Christ implied a certain challenge to the status quo, as theology began to get in touch with the margins and the real pressures of life.

In a 1908 address, Mott referred to Jesus in an attempt to put an end to the all-too-common separation of religion and politics that tends to support the powers that be: "Jesus Christ is Lord and therefore must reign. He only has authority to rule social practices. He must dominate His followers and all society in all their relationships: domestic, industrial, commercial, civic, national, and international . . . There are not two gospels, one social and one individual. There is but one Christ." The kingdom of God, Mott realized, should include "the kingdoms of finance, commerce, industry, labor, the movies, the press, learning, and of society, because Christ is to be Lord of all or He is not Lord at all." Here we encounter some ambivalence that has the potential to challenge empire, especially when Mott referred to "the larger Christ" and "larger evangelism."[59] What would happen if Christ cannot be relegated to a narrowly religious realm and if Christ is indeed somehow concerned with those on the margins and the sort of pressures that the status quo refuses to notice?

To be sure, the perspective from below tends to become more popular in times of great pressure; and the Great Depression in the United States forced people to face basic economic questions and conditions. In 1930 even the

Methodist bishops noted deep problems "with a social system that, in the midst of plenteous abundance, dooms untold numbers of our people to unbearable poverty and distress through no apparent fault of their own."[60] While the first Methodist Social Creed was adopted already at the General Conference of 1908,[61] this creed was developed further in light of the tensions of industrialized society. Subsequent embodiments of the Social Creed even became the foundation for later legislation, such as the eight-hour workday, workers' safety and compensation, Social Security, unionization, insurance, and retirement.[62] The theological surplus can be identified when these issues are seen not as merely social or political concerns (a common strategy to discount the importance of such perspectives) but as being related to the reality of God.

While the foundations of empire remained in place, the fact that Methodism mustered a theological surplus and contributed to resistance needs to be noted in our own time, when much of this is hard to imagine. Methodism did not address the greatest economic catastrophe since the Great Depression in the years 2008 and 2009 with nearly the same energy: the causes and pressures of the economic meltdown were hardly discussed, and many church people were unaware that pressures on lower-class and working-class people have increased enormously during the past decades. A stance such as the one taken by the Methodist Federation for Social Action in the 1930s sounds unimaginable now, describing itself as "an organization which seeks to abolish the profit system in order to develop a classless society based upon the obligation of mutual service."[63] Although this stance was not appreciated by everyone, it points to a theological surplus that cannot easily be captured by the status quo, as well as to a fundamental ambivalence that proves to be a challenge to any top-down power that seeks to control our lives and our images of God.

The Postcolonial Empire

Talking about a "postcolonial" empire appears, at first sight, to be counterintuitive. How can an empire exist without colonies? The U.S. military initiative in Iraq, begun in 2003, helps illustrate what is at stake. Whatever the real interests of the administration of President George W. Bush in its war against the nation of Iraq may have been, it is clear that no efforts were made to turn Iraq into a traditional colony. No U.S. governor was instituted; Iraq was to maintain its national independence as well as the ownership of its land and natural resources. At the same time, the economic benefits for the United States are substantial. While the oil reserves are owned by Iraq, U.S. companies are being awarded the rights of production; this is where the real money is made. Economically, these arrangements are much more convenient than previous colonial relations—and they are much less visible. Once military activity ceases and everything appears to be "back to normal," the public will hardly be aware of the structures of empire. Non-colonial economic relations are also more lucrative, as Adam Smith, the father of capitalism, predicted more than two centuries ago. A postcolonial empire that operates on the basis of economic ties and other links at the level of culture and media (constantly expanding through new technologies) is more effective and all encompassing than colonial models.

While some theologians may be aware of this issue, few have addressed its theological implications. Since the postcolonial empire is virtually invisible in the countries that benefit the most from it—except in times when governments engage in saber rattling of rather questionable success—few tend to notice and even fewer choose to deal with the issue. Some have even gone so far as to suggest that, since colonialism is a thing of the past, we can now go back to business as usual, in postmodern and postcolonial innocence.[64]

This brings us to one of the key features of the postcolonial situation: an increasing cover-up of the powers of empire, accompanied by an ever-further reach of those powers into our lives. Political and economic forces are joined by cultural forces (including media and technology), psychological forces (the advertising industry, for instance, seeks to impact our deepest desires), and religious forces (not just the Religious Right but other mainline ventures as well). Since the asymmetry of power is one of the hallmarks of the contemporary situation, resistance appears to be futile. In this context, the problem is not only direct support of empire. Mainline efforts at pursuing a middle road also become problematic. When power is distributed asymmetrically, those who seek to gather in the middle will inevitably be drawn in the direction of the greater pull; and, what is worse, this happens mostly without detection. It would be quite interesting to examine, for instance, Methodist historian Albert Outler's influential efforts as a centrist (working toward a "right-and-center coalition"[65]) in this light, as well as Bishop Scott Jones's notion of Methodist doctrine as the "extreme center." What does it really mean to claim, as Jones does, that "on the theological spectrum Wesley occupies the extreme center"[66] and to assume that this is the place of The United Methodist Church? What powers are covered up and left unreconstructed here, and who ultimately benefits? Wesley's approach is profoundly different: when he brought together "extremes" such as evangelism and justice ministries, or worship and social action, it was never for the sake of finding a "balance" or a "middle road." Rather, as those elements came together, a *new*, radical position emerged that was not afraid to take the side of people at the margins and to resist the status quo—producing a surplus that was bigger than the sum of its part. This points to the genius and the energy of Methodism.

A recent statement by Jones regarding the construction of a library and a partisan political institute at Southern Methodist University by the Bush Foundation in honor of President George W. Bush throws some light on the problem, which is ultimately a theological one: "I know that George W. Bush's membership in The United Methodist Church has been controversial for some in our church who disagree with his policies. Our church embraces a wide spectrum of political views and I am proud of this. I am grateful that the UMC includes both Senator Hilary Clinton and President Bush as active, faithful members. At times I disagree with both, and at times I agree with both. But they are my sister and brother in Christ, and I claim them as part of my United Methodist family."[67] Obviously this statement was written by a centrist, who saw no need to raise the bigger question of whether the positions that he qualified as extremes in this spectrum were ultimately true to the mission of the church. Membership in The United Methodist Church seemed to be sufficient; and the main task of the centrist was to find a comfortable middle ground in the context of some predetermined spectrum of political views that were all somehow acceptable. Of course neither of these views was much interested in resisting empire, despite different preferences for hard (Bush) or soft (Clinton) power. What is missing here is an awareness that not all of the places on the spectrum of the status quo of contemporary party politics may be acceptable, and that there may be legitimate places outside of this spectrum. The Methodist traditions were most powerful and meaningful precisely where they found God at work outside of the spectrum defined by the status quo: here, a theological surplus was identified that had the power to inspire Christianity as a whole and whose goal was to transform the world.

The middle road is crucial for the postcolonial empire, because it allows for undetected moves in the direction of the powers that be. In addition, it provides the kind of stability that buffers the more extreme and less successful adventures of empire, like the military efforts of the United States in recent years. Finally, the middle road guarantees that the more extreme moves of empire will stay with us for a long time to come, because they are now embedded in what is acceptable by the system. In the United States, for instance, the middle road is now further to the right than it was just a few years ago, and it will not swing back quickly, even after the aggressive politics of the Bush administration have faded. This is reflected in a report from one of the largest United Methodist churches in Texas, where it appears to be no longer acceptable even to speak of the poor; any mention of the poor is now seen as ideological. Methodist lay theologian Barbara Wendland has reported about a church newsletter that gave the title "centurions" to members who pledge several thousand dollars to the church, a title that is said to signify "the exemplary model of honorable and courageous leadership. This leadership enabled the Roman Army to achieve what many believed to be impossible."[68] When the mainline church can no longer even mention the margins of the empire (the poor), and when the Roman Empire serves once again as a role model, empire appears to have won.

Where is the theological surplus in this situation? There is plenty of resistance, much of which is not reported by the official channels. There are a substantial number of people who are on the verge of leaving or have left the church (I have met them in the United States, in Europe, in Latin America, and in Africa), not because they have lost faith, but because they have a sense that the church trivializes the Christian faith and that it has given up the search for any meaningful theological surplus that would push us beyond the confines of status quo (whether defined by Clinton, Bush, or Obama). There is a growing level of the kind of ambivalence from below that challenges both the self-confidence of the empire and the cozy middle road. Unfortunately, this is often mistaken for a lack of faith or commitment. But in a situation where notions such as the lordship of Christ and church membership are used to shore up empire, any effort to raise questions should be welcomed. Only such efforts to question will lead to a deeper sense of divine reality, which is not available to those who simply repeat mindlessly after the status quo. The challenge here is to put this sort of ambivalence to productive use and to rethink the Christian heritage in constructive fashion, understanding how our theological traditions have been shaped by empire (consciously and unconsciously), and how we can develop a deeper sense for their theological surplus.[69]

Alternatives to Empire

Recently a flier announcing a lecture promised to examine the question "whether the received gospel was the interposition of Roman governmental authorities." It is fairly safe to assume that not even the most powerful Roman governmental authorities mustered enough power to define the religion of the people. Under the conditions of postcolonial empire, it is even less the case that governmental officials can tell the churches exactly what they have to believe. But this is hardly necessary, now less than ever. The most influential powers of empire are diffuse and work best underground, at the level of the subconscious. When the empire shapes our logic, no one needs to give us an official definition of a "lord" or tell us what to understand by "love" and "justice" and how to interpret God's "omnipotence"; for the most part, empire shapes these notions unconsciously, and so its theological success is assured.

The question is whether even in this situation there is still a chance of religion not going "from the greatest to the least." Can God surprise us yet and push us beyond the theological logic of the empire or the confines of the ecclesial middle road? Is ambivalence able to point us to transcendence in fresh ways—not the ethereal "pie in the sky" type, but the kind that transcends the status quo? Is there a reality that is not determined by top-down power? Can Christianity go the other way around? In the beginnings and at some of the turning points in its history, the Methodist movement embodied this other reality. Let's see what is possible today.

| Conclusion |

A Matter of Life and Death

AS STATED EARLIER, WHEN I TELL MY STUDENTS, "THEOLOGY IS A matter of life and death," I am not talking about the importance of my field in the academy (all professors think their field is the most important one). History teaches us that theology has functioned in both ways, as life affirming and as death dealing. Too often Christianity has been on the side of the powers of death: just think of the Crusades, the conquest of the Americas, the genocide of Native Americans, chattel slavery, the German Third Reich—the list could go on. In this book, we have examined how a theology of grace can be life affirming even in the midst of great pressures and oppositions that seem insurmountable. Key to this renewed vision of grace is God's own work in church and world, preceding and empowering fresh ways of human action, human hope, and human belief.

Alternative Leadership Qualities in the Christian Tradition

Addressing the challenges of Christianity in light of the pressures of contemporary life, which are prominently shaped by the challenges of empire, may be depressing. It makes us feel like the disciples as they responded to one of Jesus' most outrageous statements, namely, that it would be easier for a camel to go through the eye of a needle than for a rich person to enter the kingdom of God: "Then who can be saved?" (Mark 10:26). Challenging empire may indeed be a bit like trying to push a camel through the eye of a needle. But let us not forget Jesus' response: "For mortals it is impossible, but not for God; for God all things are possible" (v. 27). Good news does not need to get drowned out by bad news. It may become even better news if it dares to confront the bad news with the courage of Jesus. Exegetes at times have tried to soften the story by arguing that the "eye of the needle" was a gate in the city walls of Jerusalem that made it harder, but not impossible, for camels to enter. It meant they had to get down on their knees and leave behind their baggage. But the shock of the disciples and the fact that Jesus picked up on the impossibility of this act suggest a different interpretation: it is not only difficult for the wealthy to enter the kingdom of God; it simply cannot be done. Forgive me for saying it so bluntly, but unless we address the real issues that make it impossible for us to enter the kingdom of God, the life of the church will be reduced to playing sandbox games. What is at stake here, therefore, is nothing less than the future of the church as a whole, and our hope for the world.

What is the church to do in this situation? To answer this question, we have to understand and admit that the church has become part of the problem. Empire, as the effort to control all of life, has always included religion and the church. From the beginning, the church has been tempted to join the powers that be; and this temptation only grew as the church became the official religion of the Roman Empire under Constantine in the fourth century. The church is therefore never off the hook. Even genuine efforts to build relationships with others rather than to coerce them (exemplified in the work of John R. Mott, discussed in the previous chapter) can be assimilated by empire's efforts to expand its top-down powers. Even sustained acts of sympathy, such as the learning of other people's languages, can be misused for the purposes of expansion of top-down power.[1] Contemporary mission trips and immersion experiences need to be seen in this light as well. Becoming more kind, loving, and respectful will not necessarily challenge the differentials of power so characteristic of our globalizing world.

Our Methodist traditions give us a set of clues about a different approach that has the potential to change everything. In previous chapters of this book, John Wesley's statement that "religion must not go from the greatest to the least, or the power would appear to be of men" has provided some guidance. No doubt, the power of much of what drives empire goes "from the greatest to the least," and it does indeed appear to be of men—of a group of very powerful men who could be named individually, and a few powerful women as well. Providing an alternative to this power that "would appear to be of men" is what set the Methodist movement apart from the mainline church of its time. Its most original insight, corroborated in real life, was that religion could indeed go the other way around— starting not from the top down but from the bottom up, with the "least of these." The dynamic of the Methodist movement depended on the response of common people and on whether they would become the multipliers of this message, with the help of a band of rather uneducated preachers. Methodism is not the story of one heroic leader; how could one person have possibly pulled off a revival by himself? The leadership that sustained the movement grew out of a bottom-up dynamic that was bigger than Wesley or any of the other prominent leaders.

In the midst of the empire of his own day, moving from the greatest to the least, from the British Empire to the colonies and from the emerging captains of industry to the factory floors, Wesley identified a different process that reshaped his theology and his ministry, and that is reflected in his notion of grace: meeting God at the bottom, with those at the margins and under pressure, can result in rebuilding the life of faith from the bottom up. It is for this all-important reason that he ultimately included works of mercy as means of grace, turning around the basic logic that drives Christianity. Engaging others in solidarity—through what Wesley called "works of mercy"—becomes a "channel" of God's grace, a way in which God engages us and transforms us. This initial movement that is characteristic for God's grace—from the bottom up instead of from the top down—has the potential to translate into a larger movement that resists the power grab of empire and provides for real-life alternatives.

Nevertheless, once we cease moving from the top down, we still need leaders and leadership; we still need to think about power. Rejecting the topics of leadership and power is a fairly common response by those who are fed up with the powers that be; but it will not solve anything. Indeed, it will reinforce the system already in place. The difference is that, with the sort of reversal for which the Methodist movements stand, we now have a couple of options when it comes to leadership talk and power talk. Just what are these options, if we do not want to continue moving with the current spirit of empire "from the greatest to the least"? How might it be possible to move the other way around?

The expansion of imperial power has affected Christianity throughout its history and was already a problem at the time of the apostle Paul. To be sure, the direction of Roman imperial power was "from the greatest to the least," and leadership was defined in those terms. Successful leaders would imitate the Roman emperor. They would expand the reach of imperial power through their own actions, thereby expunging any and all alternatives that could potentially challenge the empire. As recent research has shown, Paul resisted exactly that sort of thing.[2] When Paul talked about Jesus as "Lord," for example, he deliberately chose one of the key titles of the Roman emperor. But Paul used this title in a subversive way. He saw Jesus as modeling a different sort of leadership and a different kind of power than that of the Roman emperor.

The sort of leadership provided by Jesus as Lord implied a radical break with the Roman Empire and initiated a different flow of power. Whereas the Roman emperor led from the top down, Jesus led from the bottom up. "Though he was in the form of God, [he] did not regard equality with God as something to be exploited, but emptied himself, taking the form of a slave, being born in human likeness" (Phil. 2:6–7). Paul thus proclaimed "Christ crucified, a stumbling block to Jews and foolishness to Gentiles, but to those who are the called, both Jews and Greeks, Christ the power of God and the wisdom of God" (1 Cor. 1:23–24). This was reflected in the calling of the Christians, since "God chose what is foolish in the world to shame the wise; God chose what is weak in the world to shame the strong; God chose what is low and despised in the world, things that are not, to reduce to nothing things that are" (1 Cor. 1:27–28).

This was the beginning of an alternative movement that runs counter to the status quo. It cannot be understood as merely a harmless variation, as its intention is not the broadening or the enrichment of the top-down model. It is not about adding the foolish, the weak, the lowly, and despised to the status quo, which is what we often try to do when confronted with the "least of these," even in the church. This alternative movement resists and counteracts the moves from above. It shames the wise and the strong, "reducing to nothing" the status quo and business as usual, both in the church and in the world. All of this is God's choice—God's election, to use the technical theological term.

Christ's power as Lord decidedly moves from the bottom up and generates a new way of being in the world. It is this power, rather than the power of the Roman or any other empire, that has proven potent enough to spread to "all nations," lasting "to the end of the age" (Matt. 28:19–20); this is the power that was embodied once again in the Methodist movement and its efforts to transform the world (to paraphrase Wesley's notion of "spreading scriptural holiness over the land"[3]). This power does not demand the destruction of difference, as notions of leadership shaped by the spirit of empire tend to do; rather, as the image of the church as the body of Christ demonstrates, this power affirms difference by tearing down conventional power differentials: "God has so arranged the body, giving the greater honor to the inferior member" (1 Cor. 12:24).[4]

The difference between power flowing from the top down and power flowing from the bottom up appears in the traditions of the early church as well. The Nicene Creed (325 CE), for instance, can be read in both ways, and it makes a tremendous difference how it is read. The genesis of this creed reflects the top-down process of the imperial power pursued by Emperor Constantine, who made Christianity the official religion of the Roman Empire. Upon becoming sole emperor, Constantine pursued various strategies to unify the empire. Religious unification was one of them. When Constantine called the Council of Nicaea, the church became part of empire in a way that was qualitatively different from what had gone before. Never before had the church expressed doctrine through the decisions of a unified council—this used to be the way in which the empire hammered out its decrees. The New Testament canon, by contrast, witnesses to the diversity of the early church. Never before had an emperor directly suggested a key theological solution. Constantine not only called the council, funded the travel and expenses of the bishops, and presided over the sessions, but also proposed the central theological term of the Nicene Creed: the *homoousia* ("essential equality") of God and Jesus, the first and the second persons of the Trinity.

Yet the Nicene Creed can also be understood in terms of an alternative movement. It seems Constantine realized this too late, and this may well be the reason why he abandoned the Nicene Creed later and reverted to Arianism. The key to reading the Nicene Creed from the bottom up is the person of Jesus. It is striking that this creed neglects something that is at the very heart of the Christian tradition: the life and ministry of Jesus. The creed moves directly from the Incarnation to the Cross, as if what happened in between did not matter. Here we can observe a move that is typical for empire: the empire is interested in Jesus only as a God who matches the principles of classical theism, such as impassibility, immutability, and omnipotence. This means that the life and ministry of a Jewish peasant called Jesus, who was anointed by the Spirit to "bring good news to the poor . . . and recovery of sight to the blind, to let the oppressed go free"

(Luke 4:18), who "healed the sick, fed the hungry, and ate with sinners"[5] had to be effaced. Clearly, a new leadership model is proposed here that is diametrically opposed to the leadership model espoused by the Roman Empire and all subsequent empires.

But more is at stake. We are not just talking about what kind of leadership we might wish to endorse; we are talking about the nature of Godself. What the Nicene Creed says is that this Jesus really *is* God. This is what Arius, the nemesis of the Nicene Creed, feared would happen. He was worried that once Jesus was included in the Godhead, strange things would happen to Godself, so he opted for a solution that considered Jesus as very special but not quite as God. With the Nicene Creed it would no longer be possible to think about God in top-down terms, as the purely "unmoved mover" of all things. God would now have to be rethought in terms of a relationship of equals. And if the truth would get out—that Jesus was a fellow who stood for outrageous programs, such as "the last will be first, and the first will be last" (Matt. 20:16; cf. 19:30)—the character of the Godhead would never be the same.[6]

Reading the Nicene Creed from the bottom up—that is to say, from the perspective of Jesus—has radical consequences for both church and world in the context of empire. What is at stake is how we understand God—the core of reality, who created heaven and earth. Is God the one who acts from the top down and who backs up the movement of empire from the top down, as the Christian Roman empire, and all subsequent Christian empires, believed? Or is God the one who became human in Jesus Christ, who was born in a manger in a stable rather than in a cradle in a palace, in a depressed area of Palestine called Galilee, who was a day laborer in construction,[7] and who would side with the sick, the outcast, and the sinners rather than with the established and the powerful? If we can resist the efforts of empire to control the way we think and what we believe, then a whole new picture emerges—not just of Jesus but also of Godself.

This is why the Nicene Creed is so important: read from the bottom up rather than from the top down, it reminds us that God is radically different from our assumptions. The Methodist traditions, as I have shown in this book, can be understood in sync with this bottom-up reading. Yet they, too, can benefit from the theological lines that emerge from a clearer understanding of God from the bottom up. Here, more work needs to be done if the church is to make a difference today.

At the moment, the mainline church is stuck. Conservative theological positions that usually uphold the importance of the Nicene Creed never discuss the all-important reversal of top-down and bottom-up perspectives. Conservative Christians mostly move from the top down and thus end up domesticating Jesus by ignoring the clear message of the Gospels and of the apostle Paul. Whether this happens consciously or unconsciously makes no difference. Liberal theological positions, on the other hand, tend to leave the Nicene Creed in the past and tend to tone down the divinity of Jesus. As a result, they forgo the tremendous challenge that this creed poses for the church under the conditions of empire. While the Nicene Creed, read from the bottom up, encourages us to rethink God from the perspective of Jesus, liberals leave untouched the image of God at the top and the top-down theology that goes with it. As a result, both conservatives and liberals fail to challenge the image of the Divine that is at the core of globalization from the top down. And they fail to do what is most needed: to rethink the image of God.

It does not take much imagination to realize that these theological reflections have the potential to change our ideas of leadership in radical ways. Leaders are now no longer the ones who operate from the top down, telling others what to do. For good reasons, the term *servant leadership*, picking up Jesus' recommendation that those who want to be leaders must be servants, is used more and more widely these days. The term certainly points in the right direction, though it is not without its problems. The trouble with servant leadership, as it is pursued today, is that it often does not challenge top-down structures. At times it even reinforces them, as one of the more problematic assumptions about the difference between United Methodist deacons and elders shows, according to which deacons are seen more closely related to the task of "service" than elders. Even the Walmart Corporation now uses the term *servant leadership* in its management philosophy to reinforce the top-down power of its managers and top-down models of globalization.[8] In this context, we need to remember Jesus' warning that no one can serve two masters, God and "mammon" (Matt. 6:24 KJV). Read in our situation, this claim implies that we cannot have it both ways—that no one can serve empire and the church, or the free-market economy and the economy of grace, at the same time. If we try to do that, one will always win out; and there is no secret as to which one it is. What kind of leadership models would be able to turn things around to such a degree that the flow of power from the top down—the norm under the current condition of empire—is reverted?

Alternative Leadership Begins with Listening

When we neglect to listen to other voices, we often hear only ourselves. Without listening, the church and theology become narcissistic by default. At all levels of the church, from the Sunday schools to the theological academy, there is a temptation to get stuck circling around ourselves and our own interests. On the other hand, there are times when we are listening too indiscriminately. Here our efforts to think about God become market driven and determined by the powers of empire, by those who speak in the loudest voice. Alternative leadership demands that we learn *when* to listen and to *what*.

In the Methodist traditions following John Wesley, the means of grace mark the most important places where we need to listen. Means of grace, as we have seen earlier, are channels through which we receive God's grace or links through which we are connected to God and that help us sustain our relationship. Initially Wesley identified prayer, reading the Bible, and Holy Communion as the means of grace; later he added Christian conference and fasting. The older Wesley, summing up one of the most distinct contributions of Methodism to Christianity, also put strong emphasis on the works of mercy as means of grace. Each of these elements provides an opportunity for the formation of leadership in the context of listening to God and to other people. Here are five concrete steps that, in one way or another, need to be part of the formation of new leadership and a church in touch with what really matters:

Prayer. In this lineup, praying does not mean presenting God with a wish list or performing a religious ritual. Prayer is about being in dialogue with God, which means speaking as well as listening. Praying means opening up to alternative experiences of God in the midst of the pressures of life, aligning our purposes with God's purposes when the going gets tough. Jesus himself set the example in Gethsemane, aware of his pending arrest: "Not what I want, but what you want" (Mark 14:36). Praying is not only a personal matter, as Wesley was well aware; it also takes place in community. And community, in the Methodist traditions, always includes the "least of these," so that the dialogue with God is necessarily extended to include others who are pushed to the margins and experience the deepest pressures of life. If our experience of listening is not intensified in this way, we may find it impossible to listen to the divine and the church ceases to be the church.

Scripture Reading. Reading the Bible also implies listening and a dialogue. Not only do we read the Bible; the Bible also "reads us"—an insight that was one of the genuine contributions of Latin American liberation theology.[9] We are shaped in this interaction in ways that we cannot anticipate and that lead us beyond our common confinement to the stereotypical "religious" or "ecclesial" realms into interaction with all of God's creation. Like prayer, the Bible has its place not only in personal life but also in the community. Written by a large number of highly diverse people and groups, all having encountered God in their lives, the Bible cannot be understood in its full depth without being read in communities that (1) are diverse enough to capture the most severe pressures of life and (2) have made diverse encounters with God in those situations. That the unity of the biblical canon has always been a unity in diversity[10] is often overlooked though it holds a major lesson for the church.

Holy Communion. Everything comes together in the celebration of Holy Communion. Here the Bible is read, prayer and the liturgy (representing the broad traditions of the church) find their deepest roots, a community of diverse members gathers, and Christ's presence is encountered in ways that have the potential to revitalize and at times revolutionize our theological and doctrinal images.[11] The "open Table" of the Methodist tradition, inviting all who repent of their sin and want to live in peace with one another, breaks open our always too narrow images of community and extends our horizons. The community gathered around the Table in the Methodist tradition includes not only those who are official members of the church but also all who are aware of their shortcomings and seek to find new sources of life—particularly those at the margins of society who struggle along these lines but whom we often fail to take seriously as brothers and sisters because they do not fit our ecclesial profile. Such an open Table is more than a Methodist quirk. It reminds us of the fact that unless the church as a whole manages to respect and relate to others whom we see, we stand little chance of respecting and relating to the Other whom we cannot see (1 John 4:20).

Christian Conference. In this context Wesley's notion of "Christian conference" reminds us that we need to develop new forms of listening in community settings. The community is not a straitjacket where everybody is expected to think alike—demanding conformity is a pervasive problem of community formation. Instead, it is a place that creates space for discourses "seasoned with salt," as Wesley put it.[12] Wesley's questioning of conventional top-down leadership best modeled the challenges of such a discourse, which demands not conformity but courage to speak up.[13]

Fasting. Fasting, in this context, might help resist the increasing commodification of life in the twenty-first century, where everything is put up for quick consumption. Fasting might teach us that listening cannot be a mode of consumption, like watching a show on TV or picking up the latest gossip. For the church, listening has nothing to do with a voyeuristic attitude, but with opening up to the challenges of life and participating in efforts to address them in community settings.

The so-called works of mercy provide the all-important challenge in this list and take us back through each of the elements. Although works of mercy are usually identified not with an attitude of listening but with "outreach"—with being proactive and doing things for others—all of that changes radically if we follow Wesley's lead and consider the works of mercy as means of grace. In this light, working together *with* (not *for*) people under pressure and at the margins provides prime opportunities for listening. More specifically, in this context, our whole way of listening is reshaped, as we listen to people and matters that we have never before noticed and begin to understand what is worth listening to and what is not. Encountering God in this context, at the margins rather than at the top, opens us to the challenge of encountering alternative images of God in prayer, Bible, and Holy Communion. Here lies the most important and urgent lesson for the present, since the postcolonial empire is increasingly limiting our ability to listen in meaningful ways to anything and anybody who is different from us. If Wesley was concerned that people who were not aware of the works of mercy as a means of grace would fall from grace (see chap. 2), then this means we cannot be the church (or leaders of the church) without listening to others. The church stands or falls with this issue. The only way for the church to be truly the church is to keep its ears to the ground of the deepest pressures of everyday life and to wait for God there.

The formation of church leadership begins, therefore, where we least expect it. Stepping outside the artificial bubbles created by the establishment, people begin to encounter God in more real ways in situations of real pressure. These encounters with God are supported by encounters with others at the margins and under even greater pressures, opening up new approaches to prayer, the biblical writings, and Holy Communion. Here the church shows its true face, for all to see. This sort of leadership formation needs to be seen in stark contrast with what is usually considered as leadership formation today—a process that invariably proceeds from the top down even if it stresses mutuality (that "everybody can be a leader"). Without taking a stand with the margins, the default position continues to move "from the greatest to the least," so that the more educated are considered to be closer to the truth than the less educated; the powerful, more in touch with the way things are than the powerless; the wealthy, the ones to be imitated, and so on. Commonsense leadership logic finds ever-new ways to tell us that we see and judge best from the top, from the geographical elevations of mountaintops, just as well as from the upper levels of the church and society.[14]

We are only gradually beginning to realize that the reverse appears to be true—that is, that the view from below is often broader than the view from the top. The view from below usually includes the dominant perspective by default. Much of our official communication happens in the dominant language; the cultural and religious symbols of the dominant group are all-pervasive in churches and in schools; and what is "normal" is defined by people in power. Having no choice but to function in the dominant context, the view from below of necessity includes the concerns of the powers that be, nevertheless without ever being fully conformed to them.

In this context the view from below introduces a critical element. Nobody experiences more severely what is wrong with the way things are than those who are pressured by them to the point of being crushed. We need this point of view in order to evaluate where things have gone wrong and where we need to change—this is part of what it means to incorporate the works of mercy into the means-of-grace tradition. If the church is serious about listening to God for direction, it needs to learn how to listen to the whole story and how to see the larger picture, especially those parts that are silenced and usually remain invisible. The apostle Paul understood that the pain of those who are usually invisible is everyone's pain and therefore indispensable for the leadership of the church: "If one member suffers, all suffer together with it" (1 Cor. 12:26).

Leadership emerges in places where we least expect it; those who are considered to be the leaders would do well not only to acknowledge this alternative leadership, but also to be attentive to its lessons. This means two things. First, the Protestant Reformers of the sixteenth century were right when they called for the priesthood of all believers. The church has thrived on this view in ways that are not yet fully understood. This insight implies a second, and theologian Frederick Herzog has helped us see it by using the phrase the "layhood of all ministers."[15] While we need laity in positions of leadership, clergy, it should be noted, are also an integral part of the laity— literally "the people" (Greek: *laos*) of God. This insight serves as a reminder that genuine leadership must be formed in relation to all of God's people, which include those on the underside who receive little attention as well as those in official positions of leadership and power. If the body of Christ, as discussed by Paul, is the model for the true church, the common distinction between clergy and laity in terms of a distinction between leader and follower breaks down.

Here everything comes back together again: doing theology in the midst of the pressures of life—including the concern for marginalized others and the "least of these" that drove Jesus, the founders of the Christian church, and later the founders of Methodism—opens our eyes to aspects of God's reality that we have often overlooked and gives new direction and energy for leadership. If, as the writer of 1 John claimed (4:20), people who do not love their brothers and sisters cannot love God, then it must be assumed that people who fail to develop respect for other people are not able to develop respect for God. Even our grand-est theological confessions of respect for God, claiming God as "wholly Other" or as "ruler of all things," are easily pulled in by the powers that be, unless they are continuously reconstructed from below.

Conclusion

The most important characteristic of a leader is to stay in touch with the direction of God's own work in the world. What kind of leaders we become depends on how we respond to the temptation the devil set before Jesus early in his ministry: do we seek to participate in the top-down control of all the empires of the world (Matt. 4:8–10), or do we seek to pursue another way of making a difference that is grounded in alternative ways of relating to one another? The mainline church keeps forgetting that Jesus rejected the top-down way and chose the way of solidarity with the "least of these." His determination was such that the leaders of the Roman Empire (not only the Roman officials but also the Jewish high priests, who served at the pleasure of the Roman governors) felt that they had no choice but to resort to the death penalty to get rid of him. This reflects who God is and what a genuine leader is. The Methodist tradition, at its best, has picked up this lead in its beginnings; it needs to do so again in order to stay true not only to its distinct heritage, but also to its Judeo-Christian heritage.

Of course, some assume that Jesus' life and ministry were only a temporary fix and that the resurrected Christ, who "sits at the right hand of God," went on to join forces with a different power. The danger with this assumption is that it domesticates Jesus and levels the importance of the gospel narratives. It also betrays Paul's notion of the scandal of the cross and the paradoxical power that is made perfect in weakness, which he experienced (1 Cor. 1:23–25; 2 Cor. 12:8–9). It further betrays one of the basic themes of the Judeo-Christian tradition, namely, that God takes a stand against the powerful and with the humble and the meek—a position best summarized by Hannah in the Old Testament and by Mary, the mother of Jesus, in the New Testament (1 Sam. 2:1–10; Luke 1:46–55). After all, would it have been a real temptation if the devil had offered Jesus something that his Father was going to give him a short time later anyway, namely, top-down power over the world?

In theological circles concerned with leadership issues, top-down power and related top-down thinking are sometimes justified because they appear to combat relativism and an "anything goes" mentality. If a small group at the top gets to determine what is true for everyone and thus gets to set the directions for leadership, the danger of relativism may appear to be held in check. Such arrangements tend, unfortunately, to achieve the universalization of the particular relativity of a small group at the top; therefore relativism cannot be overcome from the top down.

By contrast, moving from the bottom up forces us to own up to our own relativity, but we do not need to remain stuck there. As we negotiate our differences in relationship with others without recourse to top-down power, we develop a new form of community—a sort of unity in difference—that points us beyond the traps of relativism. This is the way the Bible and the Christian traditions deal with relativity, and the church would do well to embrace this approach. In the Bible and in the Christian traditions, a truly global vision does not mean the kind of unity where everyone says exactly the same thing. Broader perspectives and truly global visions emerge when all these different voices—the many different books of the Bible written by different communities and authors over long periods of time, and the many voices of the Christian tradition, including the ones that are easily forgotten today—come together and inform one another in light of the real pressures and struggles of life.

To come to understand the good news of the gospel, finally, we need to confront the bad news. We need to face the current darkness head-on in order to understand where the light is shining brightly. The good news for both church and world is that there are real alternatives to empire, and these models are deeply rooted in our traditions, past and present. Many readers may feel, of course, that all this is too severe, that there must be some sort of a middle road between the extremes. What if the role of leadership in these times of extraordinary pressure was to lie low, to play it safe, and to refuse to get involved? As I have argued repeatedly, the problem is *there is no middle road*. No place is safe from empire as the progressive expansion of top-down power and the blotting out of alternatives. We are not even safe in the privacy of our homes and in our own minds and souls anymore; we are certainly not safe in what might be considered the privacy of our religious communities. Lying low, playing it safe, and refusing to get involved means endorsing the powers that be by default; lack of leadership can have dire consequences. Keep in mind that those who, in past manifestations of empire, attempted to pursue the middle road often discovered too late that they were drawn into the maelstrom of the system. The churches in Nazi Germany that tried to stay out of politics and retreated into their own private spheres are among the sad examples.

What is ultimately at stake, and what will make a difference in one way or another, is our image of the divine. Where do we seek God? Dietrich Bonhoeffer, the first martyr officially recognized by The United Methodist Church, believed that in order to find God we would have to look for God where God preceded us.[16] Core Judeo-Christian traditions, including the Methodist traditions, keep pointing the church and those called to be its leaders in an unmistakable direction: to the margins and to the bottom. This is where God has preceded us in Christ; it is from there that the gospel moves into the world and around the globe, to the ends of the earth—a true process of "globalization from below" that ultimately reaches all the way to the top and transforms it.[17] In this process, those who are pushed to the margins by the current dynamics of top-down power—the majority of humanity, including the majority of Christians and many Methodists—are no longer the passive recipients of the leadership schemes of the status quo. They are the ones who set the stage for a new kind of community; they become leaders in their own right, because they understand the profound meaning of the apostle Paul's insight that if one member suffers, all—the church, the world, and even Godself—suffer together with it.[18] Nothing less than the future of the church and of the world is at stake.

| Notes |

Introduction: Missing the Reality of Grace in the Church

1. For a sustained discussion of these issues as matters of theology, see Joerg Rieger, *No Rising Tide: Theology, Economics, and the Future* (Minneapolis: Fortress, 2009).

2. "Our Theological Task," *The Book of Discipline of The United Methodist Church—2008* (Nashville: The United Methodist Publishing House, 2008), 86.

3. John Wesley, "The Unity of the Divine Being," in *The Bicentennial Edition of the Works of John Wesley*, ed. Albert C. Outler (Nashville: Abingdon, 1987), 4:66; Wesley referred to a "religion of atheism," which lacks God as the true foundation. In his sermon "On Living without God," Wesley referred to "practical atheists" who do not have "God in all their thoughts"; Wesley here noted that he knew of only two individuals in Britain who denied the existence of God, and even they eventually acknowledged the existence of a merciful God. Ibid., 4:171.

4. Ernest Hemingway, *New Yorker*, November 30, 1929, quoted in John Bartlett, *Familiar Quotations*, 15th ed. (Boston: Little, Brown, 1980), 844.

Chapter 1: Methodism Thriving under Pressure

1. See, e.g., Bernard Semmel, *The Methodist Revolution* (New York: Basic Books, 1973), 192. Methodism, he says, "was among the more important reasons for this happy transition to the modern world," i.e., to liberal democracy.

2. For a reflection on Wesley's own development in terms of dealing with economic pressures, see Theodore W. Jennings, *Good News to the Poor: John Wesley's Evangelical Economics* (Nashville: Abingdon, 1990). Henry Rack, *Reasonable Enthusiast: John Wesley and the Rise of Methodism* (Philadelphia: Trinity Press, 1989), 368, argues that Wesley's concern for the social tensions of his own time was grounded in having been an "unusually well-informed observer."

3. This little-explored phenomenon transcends even denominational boundaries. Vatican II and Roman Catholic theologians such as Karl Rahner hardly disagreed

with Lutherans such as Paul Tillich or Rudolf Bultmann or with Methodists such as Albert Outler or Schubert Ogden over what constitutes the essence of modern humanity. The link between all those different theologians is, of course, not that they managed to define humanity in universal terms but that they attempted to relate to modern middle-class people and their religious sensitivities.

4. See, e.g., Albert Outler, introduction to "The Means of Grace," *The Bicentennial Edition of the Works of John Wesley*, ed. Albert C. Outler (Nashville: Abingdon, 1984), 1:377 (hereafter cited as *Works*). Wesley was less concerned, however, about having it both ways; when he brought together diverse concepts such as the means of grace and Christian praxis, something new emerges. See my argument in chap. 2.

5. For this reason, theology in the United States has never really been able to understand liberation theology. Even today, liberation theology is often still interpreted in terms of liberal theology.

6. Wesley, "Upon Our Lord's Sermon on the Mount, Eleventh Discourse," in *Works*, 1:672.

7. Ibid. Wesley no doubt has in mind mainly church people—the majority of England's population of that time.

8. This is what is missing in Albert Outler's argument that Wesley was a "folk theologian." See Albert Outler, "John Wesley: Folk Theologian," *Theology Today* 43 (July 1977): 150–60; here Outler is at pains to prove that the substance of Wesley's folk theology was deeply anchored in the learned traditions of the church. According to Outler, the point of Wesley's approach was to put these learned traditions into a popular form. It does not occur to Outler, however, that the substance of Wesley's theology itself might have also been shaped by the encounter with the people.

9. *The Journal of the Rev. John Wesley*, ed. Nehemiah Curnock (New York: Eaton and Mains, 1938): 4:52 (February 8, 1753): "On *Friday and Saturday* I visited as many more as I could, I found some in their cells under ground, others in their garrets, half starved both with cold and hunger, added to weakness and pain. But I found not one of them unemployed who was able to crawl about the room. So wickedly, devilishly false is that common objection, 'They are poor only because they are idle.'"

10. See Manfred Marquardt, *John Wesley's Social Ethics: Praxis and Principles*, trans. John E. Steely and W. Stephen Gunter (Nashville: Abingdon, 1992), 20ff. In his "Thoughts on the Present Scarcity of Provisions" of 1772, Wesley talked about various causes of poverty, including the monopolizing of farms by the "gentlemen-farmers" and the luxury of the wealthy: "Only look into the kitchens of the great, the nobility and gentry, almost without exception . . . and when you have observed the amazing waste which is made there, you will no longer wonder at the scarcity, and consequently dearness, of the things which they use so much art to destroy." *The Works of the Rev. John Wesley*, ed. Thomas Jackson, 3rd ed. (London: Wesleyan Methodist Book Room, 1872; repr. Peabody, MA: Hendrickson, 1986), 11:56–57 (hereafter cited as *Works* [Jackson]).

11. Wesley, *Works* (Jackson), 3:178.

12. Wesley, "The General Spread of the Gospel," in *Works*, 2:494. The biblical references are to Hebrews 8:11 and Romans 2:29.

13. These experiences are reflected, e.g., in Joerg Rieger, *Christ and Empire: From Paul to Postcolonial Times* (Minneapolis: Fortress, 2007), and Joerg Rieger, *No Rising Tide: Theology, Economics, and the Future* (Minneapolis: Fortress, 2009).

14. For the history of this bishops' initiative and the context of its end, see Hendrik R. Pieterse, *Opting for the Margins, Again: Recovering an Episcopal Initiative* (Nashville: General Board of Higher Education and Ministry, The United Methodist Church, 2007).

15. The Council of Bishops of the United Methodist Church, *Children and Poverty: An Episcopal Initiative* (Nashville: The United Methodist Publishing House, 1996), 7.

16. This was, e.g., Ludwig Feuerbach's point, whose argument that religion is merely a projection of our ideals matched Wesley's suspicion of middle-class religion. See Ludwig Feuerbach, *The Essence of Christianity*, trans. George Eliot (New York: Harper, 1957).

17. Feuerbach assumed that his critique was a critique of religion in general, rather than of middle-class religion.

18. Wesley's own faith was certainly influenced by his connection with the margins, but he did not include this explicitly in his own theological reflections. Here the development of theological method today needs to go beyond Wesley.

19. For the full text of the initiative, see "Children and Poverty: The Bishops' Initiative," http://archives.umc.org/initiative/statement.html.

20. That was, of course, the experience of Martin Luther, of Karl Barth, and of Latin American liberation theology.

21. The invitation to the Table is well-known: "Christ our Lord invites to his table all who love him, who earnestly repent of their sin and seek to live in peace with one another." See "A Service of Word and Table I," *United Methodist Hymnal* (Nashville: The United Methodist Publishing House, 1989), 7.

22. Wesley took very seriously his mother's report that she had been converted when participating in Holy Communion.

23. In the earlier slave trade, a slave was a sizable investment. Now the loss of slaves matters little, since there are always more to be sold. Kevin Bales, *Disposable People: New Slavery in the Global Economy* (Berkeley: University of California Press, 1999), 4.

24. See Rieger, *No Rising Tide*, 9. The fact that top executives earn four hundred to five hundred times more than average workers pales in comparison to the fact that top investors earn twenty thousand times more than average workers.

25. This theme is developed further and in reference to Protestant theology since Schleiermacher in Joerg Rieger, *God and the Excluded: Visions and Blindspots in Contemporary Theology* (Minneapolis: Fortress, 2001).

26. I deal with this question of truth in my book *Remember the Poor: The Challenge to Theology in the Twenty-First Century* (Harrisburg: Trinity Press, 1998); see, e.g., chap. 3.

27. *The Book of Discipline of The United Methodist Church—2008* (Nashville: The United Methodist Publishing House, 2008), 74.

28. One of the most blatant examples of this can be found in Friedrich Schleiermacher, *The Christian Faith*, eds. H. R. Mackintosh and J. S. Stewart (Edinburgh: T. & T. Clark, 1986), 450: "Even if it cannot be strictly proved that the Church's power of miracles has died out . . . in view of the great advantage in power and civilization which the Christian peoples possess over the non-Christian . . . the preachers of to-day do not need such signs."

29. "Canada Experiences Hunger Pains," March 10, 2005, World Vision Canada, http://www.worldvision.ca/About-Us/Newsroom/press-releases/North-America/Pages/Canadaexperienceshungerpains.aspx.

Chapter 2: Means of Grace under Pressure

1. Ole E. Borgen, *John Wesley and the Sacraments: A Theological Study* (Nashville: Abingdon, 1972), 281.

2. John Wesley, "The Means of Grace," in *The Bicentennial Edition of the Works of John Wesley*, ed. Albert C. Outler (Nashville: Abingdon, 1984), 1:381 (hereafter cited as *Works*).

3. Ibid. The three notions of Scripture, prayer, Holy Communion have a sound basis in the official Anglican formularies, Prayer Book, Ordinal, Homilies, and the Catechism.

4. John Wesley, "Minutes of Several Conversations between the Rev. Mr. Wesley and Others, from the Year 1744 to 1789," in *The Works of John Wesley*, ed. Thomas Jackson, 3rd. ed. (London: Wesleyan Methodist Book Room, 1872; repr. Peabody, MA: Hendrickson, 1986), 8:322–23 (hereafter cited as *Works* [Jackson]).

5. See Wesley, "The Means of Grace," in *Works*, 1:378.

6. The latest book dedicated to the means of grace still addresses precisely this dilemma. See Henry H. Knight III, *The Presence of God in the Christian Life: John Wesley and the Means of Grace*, Pietist and Wesleyan Studies 3 (Metuchen, NJ, and London: Scarecrow Press, 1992).

7. On Wesley's emphasis on the primacy of God's love, see, e.g., "The Witness of the Spirit, I," in *Works*, 1:274. See also "The Law Established through Faith, II," in *Works*, 2:42.

8. Wesley, "On Zeal," in *Works*, 3:313.

9. Wesley listed some of those fruits of the Spirit that Paul mentioned in Galatians 5:22–23, "long-suffering, gentleness, meekness, goodness, fidelity, temperance."

10. Wesley, "On Zeal," in *Works*, 3:314. Borgen missed this point when he emphasized the works of piety, commenting that they were "of the greatest importance for Wesley." Borgen, *John Wesley and the Sacraments*, 105.

11. *The Book of Discipline of The United Methodist Church—2008* (Nashville: The United Methodist Publishing House, 2008), 72–74. In the first two parts of the General Rules we find an extended list of what Wesley considered works of mercy.

12. Ibid., 73.

13. Knight, *Presence of God in the Christian Life*, 13, has defined works of mercy as means of grace "which encourage openness to the presence of God," as opposed to means that "describe the character and activity of God." According to Knight, God's character is described by Scripture, preaching, Eucharist, and "prayers of the tradition."

14. George E. Tinker, *Missionary Conquest: The Gospel and Native American Cultural Genocide* (Minneapolis: Fortress, 1993), 3, 17, 112.

15. Robert Allen Warrior, "A Native American Perspective: Canaanites, Cowboys, and Indians," in *Voices from the Margin: Interpreting the Bible in the Third World*, ed. R. S. Sugirtharajah (Maryknoll, NY: Orbis, 1991), 288.

16. See Wesley, "On Visiting the Sick," in *Works*, 3:385.

17. For Wesley, works of mercy were not just "prudential" in the sense that they would be optional means of grace, which may or may not be used according to changing circumstances. It has often been overlooked that Wesley's distinction between "instituted" and "prudential" means of grace does not apply here, for works of mercy are not listed in either category. See Wesley, "Minutes of Several Conversations," in *Works* (Jackson), 8:323–24. Henry Knight, too, overlooks this fact; see *Presence of God in the Christian Life*, 5.

18. See, e.g., Knight, *Presence of God in the Christian Life*, and Borgen, *John Wesley and the Sacraments*.

19. There seems to be a connection between this theological analysis and the findings of a study by the Pew Research Center that "religious teachings have remarkably little influence in shaping people's attitudes on broad social issues like welfare and the role of women in the workplace." Quoted in Gustav Niebuhr, "Politics: The Churches; Public Supports Political Voice for Churches," *New York Times*, June 25, 1996.

20. Wesley, "Upon Our Lord's Sermon on the Mount: Discourse the Thirteenth," in *Works*, 1:688–89.

21. Outler, footnote to John Wesley, "The Repentance of Believers," in *Works*, 1:343, n. 65.

22. Outler, introduction to *Works*, 1:67. See also Albert Outler, "John Wesley: Folk Theologian," *Theology Today* 34 (July 1977): 150–60.

23. For a discussion of the difference between what is now called "contextual theology" and liberation theology, see my essay "Developing a Common Interest Theology from the Underside," in *Liberating the Future: God, Mammon, and Theology*, ed. Joerg Rieger (Minneapolis: Fortress, 1998), 124–41.

24. See the work of Frederick Herzog, and my "Whaling Our Way into the Twenty-First Century," in *Theology from the Belly of the Whale: A Frederick Herzog Reader*, ed. Joerg Rieger (Harrisburg, PA: Trinity Press, 1999), 14–15.

25. Wesley, "Upon Our Lord's Sermon on the Mount: Discourse the Thirteenth," in *Works*, 1:697. See also the conclusion of Wesley's sermon "On Zeal," in *Works*, 3:321: "For 'God is love; and he that dwelleth in love, dwelleth in God and God in him' (1 John 4:16)."

26. Theodore Runyon has argued that the notions of orthodoxy and orthopraxis are tied together by a third term: *orthopathy*. Theodore Runyon, "A New Look at

'Experience,'" *Drew Gateway* (Fall 1987): 44–55. But, contrary to Runyon's intention, this emphasis might still wind up focusing on the Christian self "feeling its religious pulse."

27. See Wesley, "Upon Our Lord's Sermon on the Mount: Discourse the Eighth," in *Works*, 1:629.

28. The crucial issue of the concrete shape of Wesley's praxis, together with his concern for the poor, was neglected in Randy L. Maddox, "John Wesley—Practical Theologian?" Wesleyan *Theological Journal* 23 (1988): 101–11.

29. See Wesley, "Upon Our Lord's Sermon on the Mount: Discourse the Eighth," in *Works*, 1:629.

30. M. Douglas Meeks, "Introduction: On Reading Wesley with the Poor," in *The Portion of the Poor: Good News to the Poor in the Wesleyan Tradition*, ed. M. Douglas Meeks (Nashville: Abingdon, 1995), 9. See also the contributions of the various authors in the Meeks volume.

Chapter 3: The Economics of Grace in Global Capitalism

1. *The Book of Discipline of The United Methodist Church—2008* (Nashville: The United Methodist Publishing House, 2008), par. 120, p. 87.

2. For an investigation of free-market capitalism and its theological implications, see Joerg Rieger, *No Rising Tide: Theology, Economics, and the Future* (Minneapolis: Fortress, 2009).

3. In the United States the practice of working several jobs is quite common in lower-income communities. In these communities it is simply taken for granted that both husband and wife are employed.

4. See the numbers in Rieger, *No Rising Tide*, 9, with reference to Sarah Anderson and others, Executive Excess 2007: *The Staggering Social Cost of U.S. Business Leadership* (Washington, DC: Institute for Policy Studies and United for a Fair Economy), 9, at http://www.ips-dc.org/reports/executive_excess_2007. In 2006 the average CEO made 364 times more than an average worker in the United States, down from over 500 times a few years earlier. At the same time, the difference between the salary of an average worker and the top twenty private-equity and hedge-fund managers in the United States was much higher; the latter earned 22,255 times the pay of the average worker.

5. This was, of course, Augustine's description of Pelagius's position. See Augustine, "On the Grace of Christ," in *Theological Anthropology, Sources in Early Christian Thought*, trans. and ed. J. Patout Burns (Philadelphia: Fortress, 1981), 63.

6. The classical economic problem of scarcity that Douglas Meeks (*God the Economist: The Doctrine of God and Political Economy* [Minneapolis: Augsburg Fortress, 1989], 12, 17–18) and Stephen Long (*Divine Economy: Theology and the Market* [London: Routledge, 2000], 4, 242–44) have found at the root of the logic of the market economy is not necessarily the problem at this level. In fact, the phenomenon that I am describing shows that a logic of abundance and gift, which both Meeks and Long have seen as a

remedy for the market economy, is now also a pervasive element in certain sectors of the economy. Josef Pieper was on the right track when he defined the essence of bourgeois living as "taking for granted," and Matthew Fox has noted about this attitude that "our lives are filled with assumptions about the universe serving us all the time." See Matthew Fox, *Creation Spirituality: Liberating Gifts for the Peoples of the Earth* (San Francisco: HarperCollins, 1991), 92; the reference to Pieper can be found on the same page.

7. Wesley, in his own way, was aware of this bifurcation of activism and piety. See chap. 2.

8. John Wesley, "Upon Our Lord's Sermon on the Mount: Discourse the Thirteenth," in *The Bicentennial Edition of the Works of John Wesley*, ed. Albert C. Outler (Nashville: Abingdon, 1984), 1:697 (hereafter cited as *Works*).

9. Wesley, "On Working out Our Own Salvation," in *Works*, 3:208.

10. Thomas Langford emphasized the fact that for Wesley grace was personal, tied to the presence of God in Jesus Christ. "In a basic sense, grace is Jesus Christ." Thomas A. Langford, *Practical Divinity: Theology in the Wesleyan Tradition* (Nashville: Abingdon, 1983), 24, 48.

11. Theodore Runyon has made a similar point about Wesley's understanding of the image of God. Wesley saw this image relationally, "not so much as something humans possess as the way they relate to God and live out that relation in the world." Theodore Runyon, *The New Creation: John Wesley's Theology Today* (Nashville: Abingdon, 1998), 13.

12. In this sense, Christianity does not depend on a "metaphysics of presence." This key term of postmodern thought was coined by Jacques Derrida in his critique of philosophical systems that guarantee firm foundations for philosophical reflection. See Jacques Derrida, "Structure, Sign and Play," in *Critical Theory Since 1965*, eds. Hazard Adams and Leroy Searle (Tallahassee: University Press of Florida, 1986), 84.

13. Wesley, "The Good Steward," in *Works*, 2:283.

14. Wesley, "The New Creation," in *Works*, 2:510.

15. See Joerg Rieger, *God and the Excluded: Visions and Blindspots in Contemporary Theology* (Minneapolis: Fortress, 2001).

16. This is one of the key points of my book *No Rising Tide*. While the economy goes in cycles and tides flow and ebb, more and more people, including many members of the middle class, do not experience the rising tide anymore. It is simply not true that a rising tide lifts all boats.

17. Wesley, "On Visiting the Sick," in *Works*, 3:385.

18. See my book *Remember the Poor: The Challenge to Theology in the Twenty-First Century* (Harrisburg, PA: Trinity Press, 1998), chap. 3, where I develop a similar argument by looking at what encounters with repressed people might do in terms of new direction and new energy.

19. Wesley, "The Scripture Way of Salvation," in *Works*, 2:156.

20. This is what interested Wesley most in talking about the Methodist movement. See, e.g., his account of the Methodist movement in "On God's Vineyard," in *Works*, 3:503–17.

21. This was quite literally spelled out in Wesley's sermon "The New Creation." See *Works*, 2:510.

22. See also the essays in *Methodist and Radical: Rejuvenating a Tradition*, ed. Joerg Rieger and John Vincent (Nashville: Kingswood Books, 2004).

Chapter 4: Empire and Grace

1. For an account of Las Casas along these lines, see Joerg Rieger, *Christ and Empire: From Paul to Postcolonial Times* (Minneapolis: Fortress, 2007), chap. 4.

2. See ibid., chapter 2.

3. John Wesley, *Journal*, in *The Works of John Wesley*, ed. Thomas Jackson, 3rd ed. (London: Wesleyan Methodist Book Room, 1872; repr. Peabody, MA: Hendrickson, 1986), 21:466 (May 25, 1764).

4. This insight foreshadowed what the recent academic field of cultural studies seeks to investigate: the multiple relationships between cultural (and religious) forces and power.

5. John Walch, "Elie Halévy and the Birth of Methodism," *Transactions of the Royal Historical Society* 5, no. 25 (1975): 19.

6. See Theodore Jennings, "John Wesley," in *Empire and the Christian Tradition: New Readings of Classical Theologians*, eds. Kwok Pui-lan, Don Compier, and Joerg Rieger (Minneapolis: Fortress, 2007), 257–70. As Jennings has pointed out, Wesley noted the problems of greed, both individual and corporate, but also understood empire as a more collective matter of national policy (265).

7. The first stanza (related to Matthew 16:21) was published in *The Poetical Works of John and Charles Wesley*, vol. 10, ed. G. Osborn (London: Wesleyan-Methodist Conference Office, 1871), 301. The second stanza (related to John 7:48) was published in volume 11, 411–12, which came out the same year (edited, again, by Osborn), from the Wesleyan-Methodist Conference. Both volumes are now available on the web: http://books.google.com/books?id=Lw8DAAAAQAAJ&prints ec=frontcover&dq=bibliogroup:%22The+poetical+works+of+John+and+Charles+ Wesley,+collected+and+arranged+by+G.+Osborn%22&cd=3#v=onepage&q= &f=false.

8. *Songs for the Poor: Hymns by Charles Wesley*, ed. S. T. Kimbrough, Jr. (New York: General Board of Global Ministries, The United Methodist Church, 1993).

9. Sometimes Wesley seemed to have given up on those at the top altogether, although the bottom-up directionality of religion remained. He advised his preachers: "Do not affect the gentleman. You have no more to do with this character than with that of a dancing master." Cited in Umphrey Lee, *The Lord's Horseman: John Wesley the Man* (Nashville: Abingdon, 1954), 115. In a letter to Freeborn Garretson on September 30, 1786, Wesley noted, "[T]he poor are the Christians. I am quite out of conceit with almost all those who have this world's goods." *The Letters of the Rev. John Wesley*, ed. John Telford (London: Epworth Press, 1931), 7:343–44.

10. See Rieger, *Christ and Empire*; Joerg Rieger, "Christian Theology and Empires," in *Empire and the Christian Tradition*, 1–14.

11. For a discussion of the concept of surplus and its theoretical roots, see Rieger, *Christ and Empire*, 9.

12. For the notion of "ambivalence," see Homi Bhabha, *The Location of Culture* (London: Routledge, 1994), 86. Bhabha connected this term with his more famous notion of mimicry: "the discourse of mimicry is constructed around an *ambivalence*" (emphasis in original). By repeating colonial images (with a slight difference), rather than representing them accurately, mimicry establishes a challenge to the colonial narcissism and fiction of self-identity (88). This notion of ambivalence is a central concept in my book *Christ and Empire*.

13. Ibid., 88; italics in original. While Bhabha saw the ambivalence of mimicry as a surface effect and did not want to relate it too closely to the Freudian notion of the "return of the repressed," I do not think that these matters are mutually exclusive. For an effort to read Bhabha's work in relation to the notion of repression, see my essay "Liberating God-Talk: Postcolonialism and the Challenge of the Margins," in *Postcolonialism Theologies*, eds. Catherine Keller, Michael Nausner, and Mayra Rivera (St. Louis: Chalice, 2004).

14. David Hempton, *Methodism: Empire of the Spirit* (New Haven, CT: Yale University Press, 2005), 210.

15. Ibid., 128. On page 203, Hempton has listed the following dialectical tensions, going back to Wesley himself: between discipline and emotions, work ethic and ritual, emancipation for the oppressed and an "unrelenting bourgeois ethic of acquisitiveness."

16. Ibid., 87.

17. John Walch noted that "in a variety of ways Methodism was an active solvent of patriarchal deference. There was a wide gap between its political theory and the situational reality of continual collision with the representatives of the established order." Walch, "Elie Halévy and the Birth of Methodism," 19.

18. Hempton, *Methodism*, 87.

19. Ibid., 131–32.

20. E. P. Thompson, *The Making of the English Working Class* (New York: Vintage Books, 1966), 37.

21. Ibid., 42.

22. David Hempton, *The Religion of the People: Methodism and Popular Religion c. 1750–1900* (London: Routledge, 1996), 173.

23. Thompson, *Making of the English Working Class*, 401, put it this way: "Methodism and Utilitarianism, taken together, make up the dominant ideology of the Industrial Revolution" (see also 375, 391). While seeking to challenge Thompson's work, even Hempton (*Religion of the People*, 169) conceded this clear awareness of the tensions to be the genius of Thompson's work. Hempton stressed the positive side of the tensions, while Thompson identified the problems.

24. A. Gregory Schneider, *The Way of the Cross Leads Home: The Domestication of American Methodism* (Bloomington: Indiana University Press, 1993), 207.

25. Ibid., 208.

26. W. R. Ward notes the importance of the "priesthood of all believers" in unsettling the status quo. W. R. Ward, "Pastoral Office and the General Priesthood in the Great Awakening," *Studies in Church History* 26 (1989): 303–27.

27. Hempton, *Religion of the People*, 7.

28. Ken Bedell, "John Wesley, Empire, and Paradise," 19 (unpublished background paper for the Workgroup on Ethics, Economics, and Globalization, Oxford Institute of Methodist Theological Studies, Christ Church, Oxford University, 2007).

29. See Stephen Hatcher, "The Radicalism of Primitive Methodism," in *Methodist and Radical: Rejuvenating a Tradition*, eds. Joerg Rieger and John Vincent (Nashville: Kingswood Books, 2004), 128.

30. It should be noted, however, that Native Americans have reminded us that colonization is not over as long as internal colonization continues.

31. The role of education has been noted, e.g., by José Míguez Bonino, "Methodism and Latin American Liberation Movements," in *Methodist and Radical*, 199. This emphasis on education became the hallmark of Methodist missions; see Hempton, *Methodism*, 157. Already in 1897, John R. Mott noted the importance of educational missions in the context of India: "Educational missions have opened a larger number of doors for the preaching of the gospel than any other agency." John R. Mott, *Strategic Points in the World's Conquest: The Universities and Colleges as Related to the Progress of Christianity* (New York: Fleming H. Revell, 1897), 96.

32. Rieger, *Christ and Empire*, chap. 7.

33. Hempton, *Methodism*, 30.

34. Ibid., 152; also page 158, sums things up in terms of the two different imperialisms at work: "Methodism mapped the world on the back of two expanding civilizations. The first, the British, was to begin with an informal then a formal empire within which Methodism made its way through soldiers, sailors, migrants, traders, civilizers, and colonial governors. The second, the American, was an expansionist commercial empire, which sucked in migrants from all over the world and exported traders, educators, and doctors."

35. Ibid., 31.

36. See ibid., 102ff.

37. See ibid., 109, 125ff.

38. Dana L. Robert, "The Methodist Struggle over Higher Education in Fuzhou, China, 1877–1883," *Methodist History* 34 (April 1996): 173–89.

39. Hempton, *Methodism*, 168, 177.

40. Whereas the social gospel movement in the United States asserted "the Christian law" or the "kingdom of God," Mott asserted the lordship of Christ. See C. Howard Hopkins, *John R. Mott 1865–1955: A Biography* (Geneva: World Council of Churches; Grand Rapids: Eerdmans, 1979), 276.

41. John R. Mott, *Strategic Points in the World's Conquest: The Universities and Colleges as Related to the Progress of Christianity* (Chicago: Student Volunteer Movement for Foreign Missions, 1897), 213.

42. John R. Mott, "The Obligation of This Generation to Evangelize the World" (address to the Ecumenical Missionary Conference in New York, 1900), referenced in Frederick A. Norwood, *The Story of American Methodism* (Nashville: Abingdon, 1974), 339. Norwood also noted how this call resonated around the world.

43. David J. Bosch, *Transforming Mission: Paradigm Shifts in Theology of Mission* (Maryknoll, NY: Orbis, 1991), 324, 337; Hopkins, *John R. Mott*, 274.

44. Bosch, *Transforming Mission*, 296.

45. Ibid., 324–25.

46. Ibid., 301.

47. Ibid., 302.

48. John R. Mott, *Cooperation and the World Mission* (New York: International Missionary Council, 1935), 28.

49. Hempton, *Methodism*, 168.

50. Mott, *Strategic Points in the World's Conquest*, 20, 30–31, 34.

51. Bosch, *Transforming Mission*, 465.

52. Mott, *Cooperation and the World Mission*, 15, 29.

53. "One of the most nobly useful men in the world," was President Wilson's assessment of Mott in 1914 (quoted in Hopkins, *John R. Mott*, 435). The funding sources for Mott's projects were tremendous. The extremely wealthy, including the robber barons and their heirs, "trusted him to spend, or invest, a part of their surplus in instrumentalities dedicated to human betterment through religious agencies." Ibid., 51.

54. Quoted in Norwood, *Story of American Methodism*, 347.

55. See Hempton, *Methodism*, 46–47.

56. Norwood, *Story of American Methodism*, 399.

57. Ibid., 400.

58. Quoted in Hopkins, *John R. Mott*, 275.

59. Quoted in ibid., 628.

60. Quoted in Norwood, *Story of American Methodism*, 400.

61. Ibid., 353–54, 391.

62. At the beginning of the nineteenth century, the workday was ten hours, six days a week. However, before things got better, the workday had increased to seventy hours a week, and unionization and collective bargaining were opposed. See ibid., 399.

63. Ibid., 393.

64. See, e.g., the approach of Bosch, *Transforming Mission*, who has thoroughly examined the failures of mission under colonialism, yet somehow assumes that these times are behind us. For a fuller account of this oversight, see my essay "Theology and Mission in a Postcolonial World," *Mission Studies: Journal of the International Association for Mission Studies* 21, no. 2 (2004): 201–27. I am not arguing against

mission as such. My point is that we need to become aware of the current asymmetries of power before we can take up the matter again.

65. This term was used in one of Albert Outler's letters to Pastor Ed Robb, reproduced in Riley B. Case, *Evangelical and Methodist: A Popular History* (Nashville: Abingdon, 2004), 220.

66. Scott J. Jones, *United Methodist Doctrine: The Extreme Center* (Nashville: Abingdon, 2002), 19. Jones has assumed that a middle road exists between worship and social action, evangelism and justice ministries, spiritual formation and political involvement.

67. Scott J. Jones, e-mail sent to 120 bishops of The United Methodist Church in January 2007. For a news report see the Web site of The United Methodist Church, "Controversy Intensifies over Proposed Bush Library at SMU," dated January 19, 2007: http://www.umc.org/site/apps/nl/content3.asp?c=lwL4KnN1LtH&b=2429867&ct=3456005.

68. Barbara Wendland, *Connections* 178 (August 2007): 1.

69. This is the project of my book *Christ and Empire*, where I seek to reclaim Paul's notion of the lordship of Christ, the insistence of Christ's full divinity and humanity as developed in the Councils of Nicaea and Chalcedon; Anselm's notion of the God-human; Las Casas's notion of the Way of Christ; Schleiermacher's appropriation of Christ as prophet, priest, and king; Aulén's *Christus Victor*; and Matthew Fox's Cosmic Christ.

Conclusion: A Matter of Life and Death

1. Bartolomé de Las Casas was one example of this approach. See my assessment in *Christ and Empire: From Paul to Postcolonial Times* (Minneapolis: Fortress, 2007), chap. 4.

2. See, e.g., Richard Horsley, ed., *Paul and the Roman Imperial Order* (Harrisburg, PA: Trinity Press, 2004); John Dominic Crossan and Jonathan L. Reed, *In Search of Paul: How Jesus' Apostle Opposed Rome's Empire with God's Kingdom* (San Francisco: HarperSanFrancisco, 2004). For an overview and an interpretation from a theological perspective, see Rieger, *Christ and Empire*, chap. 1.

3. The reference is to John Wesley's Large Minutes of 1763, where he talked about the Methodist task "to reform the nation and, in particular the Church; to spread scriptural holiness over the land."

4. For a more detailed account of Paul's approach, see Rieger, *Christ and Empire*, chap. 1.

5. This language, taken from the accounts of the New Testament, is part of the United Methodist liturgy. See "A Service of Word and Table Service I," *The United Methodist Hymnal* (Nashville: The United Methodist Publishing House, 1989), 9.

6. For a more detailed account, see Rieger, *Christ and Empire*, chap. 2.

7. See Mark 6:3: *tektōn* is the Greek word often translated as "carpenter."

8. See "Servant Leadership" on the Walmart Web site: http://walmartstores.com/About Us/289.aspx. Servant leaders, we are told, are managers who "don't lead

from behind a desk" and thus create "wonderful morale." While "listening" is a quality of servant leaders at Walmart, there is no comment about the actual sharing of power. In fact, Walmart opposes the Employee Free Choice Act (H.R. 800, § 1041) that would allow employees to join unions.

9. See Gustavo Gutierrez, *We Drink from Our Own Wells: The Spiritual Journey of a People*, trans. Matthew J. O'Connell (Maryknoll, NY: Orbis, 1984), 34. This reflects the experience of the Christian Base Communities in Latin America.

10. The German exegete Ernst Käsemann has argued that the biblical canon is the foundation not of the unity of the church but of its diversity. See his "Begründet der neutestamentliche Kanon die Einheit der Kirche?" in *Exegetische Versuche und Besinnungen* (Göttingen: Vandehoeck & Ruprecht, 1960), 1:221.

11. See Joerg Rieger, *Remember the Poor: The Challenge to Theology in the Twenty-First Century* (Harrisburg: Trinity Press, 1998), 213–15.

12. John Wesley, "Minutes of Several Conversations between the Rev. Mr. Wesley and Others, from the Year 1744 to 1789," in *The Works of John Wesley*, ed. Thomas Jackson, 3rd. ed. (London: Wesleyan Methodist Book Room, 1872; repr. Peabody, MA: Hendrickson, 1986), 8:377.

13. It is well known that Wesley's own leadership style showed authoritarian tendencies, pointing to some of his own limits. At the same time, however, Wesley's leadership was not driven by the concerns of the wealthy and the powerful—and taking a stance with the marginalized always demands determination.

14. The *Rich Dad, Poor Dad* book series by Robert T. Kiyosaki, which, to promote financial success, contrasts financial advice of the rich and the poor, may be too blatant an example for this, but the popularity of the message is hard to discount. Kiyosaki's book *Rich Dad, Poor Dad: What the Rich Teach Their Kids about Money—That the Poor and the Middle Class Do Not* (New York: Warner Books, 1997) has become the best-selling personal finance book of all time.

15. Frederick Herzog, *God-Walk: Liberation Shaping Dogmatics* (Maryknoll, NY: Orbis, 1988), 129.

16. This is how Bonhoeffer's friend and biographer Eberhard Bethge summarized his theology. See Eberhard Bethge, *Dietrich Bonhoeffer: Man of Vision, Man of Courage* (New York: Harper, 1970), 771.

17. For more on the notion of "globalization from below," see Joerg Rieger, *Globalization and Theology*, Horizons in Theology (Nashville: Abingdon, 2010).

18. For a systematic and theological development of this issue, see Joerg Rieger, "Developing a Common Interest Theology from the Underside," in *Liberating the Future: God, Mammon, and Theology*, ed. Joerg Rieger (Minneapolis: Fortress, 1998), 124–41.

| Index |